Merry Christmas, ...
We hope you enjoy "Echo..."
With much love — Mel & ...
the year of the
Christmas '94

Echoings

From the Bible
in Literature

Meditations for Today

J. Ruth Stenerson

LangMarc Publishing
San Antonio, Texas

Echoings

From the Bible in Literature
Meditations for Today

By J. Ruth Stenerson

Editor: Renée Hermanson
Cover Artist: Carolyn McBride
Technical Design: Michael Qualben

Published by LangMarc Publishing
Box 33817, San Antonio, Texas 78265

Library of Congress Cataloging-in-Publication Data
Stenerson, Ruth.
      Echoings / Ruth Stenerson.
             p.   cm.
      Includes bibliographical references and index
      ISBN 1-880292-11-4 (pbk.) : $11.95
      1. Meditations.   I. Title
BV4832.2.S75   1993
242—dc20   93-9833
                                              CIP

J. Ruth Stenerson

Ruth Stenerson is Professor Emerta of English, Bemidji State University, a free-lance writer, and author of three books in the Augsburg/Fortress' Bible Readings series. Tens of thousands of people have had the rich experience of reading her *Bible Readings for Singles, Bible Readings for Teachers,* and *Bible Readings for Students.* Her graduate degree is from the University of North Dakota and her bachelor's degree is from Concordia College in Moorhead, Minnesota. She resides in Bemidji, Minnesota.

About Echoings

"In an age when many believe they are "on their own" in finding a relevant spirituality, it is a delight to discover a resource that feeds the mind as well as the soul. Ruth Stenerson touches the deepest parts of the human soul by drawing upon the Biblical witness, and skillfully interweaving the resources of our literary heritage, everyday life, and our faith traditions. Even the challenges that close each section are realistic and potentially life changing."—*Reverend Margaret J. Thomas, Executive Director, Minnesota Council of Churches.*

"'The echoes' that have inspired these meditations are insightful and creative. Readers are repeatedly challenged to articulate their faith and then to share their stories with others. The author has provided a wonderfully refreshing devotional that is accessible for all ages."—*Reverend Mark Knutson, University Chaplain, California Lutheran College.*

"Ruth Stenerson presents here a fine series of meditations. She offers her own reflection on the subject, presenting the reader with challenging ideas. This is Ruth Stenerson at her very best."—*Philip R. Sauer, Professor Emeritus of English, Bemidji State University.*

"A thought-provoking book which challenges the reader to re-evaluate his/her own faith in light of concrete suggestions made by the writer. This is the kind of book one longs to discuss with a good friend. Thoughtful readers will appreciate the many literary references which encourage further reading."—*Tekla Bekkedal, Professor Emerita, University of Wisconsin.*

"In *Echoings* the fabric of each meditation is woven with Biblical and literary references and then richly edged by prayer and a thoughtful, practical challenge. We are variously caught with our judgmental attitudes showing, prodding to listen quietly and always encouraged to respond in loving ways to others." —*Dr. Paul J. Dovre, President, Concordia College, Moorhead, MN.*

"In *Echoings*, Ms. Stenerson combines her own faith, her keen understanding of the Bible, and her extensive knowledge of the world's great literature. The result is a fresh, poignant, challenging interchange for any of us who claim and proclaim God's reality in our lives. Reading these meditations became an exciting encounter for my mind and spirit. I anticipate this book will remain a valued and favorite resource. By title, content and style, *Echoings* is good reading for the thinker in each of us and good stimulant for our spiritual beings."—*A. Keith Malmquist, Professor Emeritus of Visual Arts, Bemidji State University.*

Dedication

To everyone with whom
I share the pleasure of Bible Study and
Especially my Monday Morning Ecumenical Group

*With best wishes
that you will find
this book worthwhile.*

Ruth Stenerson

Introduction

As an inveterate reader and teacher of literature, I have for a long time observed how often the thoughts expressed in Scripture are echoed by the great writers of ancient through contemporary times. Surely that has something to say about the way in which the Scriptures speak with universality about those issues that are always on the minds of thoughtful men and women.

That manner in which Biblical writers and later ones speak to human concerns is the basis from which these devotionals grow. Each of the one hundred selections suggests a Bible reading—which of course is the best and most important part of it, with one verse chosen as focus. Please read the Bible passage. It will illuminate the rest. Each selection also has a quotation chosen from literature. Out of the relationship between the verse and the quotation the meditation grows, as does the prayer and the challenge.

Almost all of us find other human beings fascinating. In that lies much of our attraction to literature—and to the marvelous stories of Scripture. These were written, we are told, for our inspiration and instruction, as is so evident in the stories Jesus told.

You may not see in these quotations—Scriptural or otherwise—exactly the same as I have. But I hope you fill wind something stimulating and thought-provoking, ideas we can use to encourage us to see in the Bible what illuminates our own lives.

Please be sure to read the Scripture selections before you read the meditation. Those words are more important than mine.

Invitation to Prayer

"Lord, teach us to pray, just as John taught his disciples" (Luke 11:1).

"Step softly, under snow or rain,
To find the place where men can pray;...."

G. I. Chesterton

Sometimes, in our desire to appropriate the power of prayer in our lives, we make of prayer such a complicated and rule-bound activity, so hedged with "beware lest" and "but remember," that its joyousness and confident faith are all but lost. We forget how directly and naturally Jesus responds to his disciples when they ask, "Lord, teach us to pray."

Prayer was nothing new to the disciples of Jesus. Prayer was a traditional part of Judaism: its Scriptures, our Old Testament, were saturated with it. Especially the book of Psalms which was used in worship as one prayer after another. Why, then, should these Jews ask to be taught to pray? Why did John need to teach his disciples to pray?

These disciples had often watched Jesus pray in their life with him. There must have been something special about the way he prayed that convinced them that here was One who knew how to tap the power of God, not in an endless stream of words but in deep-felt intensity, not always one request after another but in expressions of praise and glad recognition of who his father was. If only he would teach them to pray like that! "Lord, teach us to pray."

There are two parts to Jesus' response to their request. First, he gives them a model prayer, one so simple that a small child can learn it, yet of such depth

1

that theologians can never plumb it fully. It speaks profoundly of the Father's name and glory, and of the basic needs of the pray-er. Second, in Jesus' usual fashion, he tells them a story, a story of a persistent person who in his need does not hesitate to upset his friend's household in order that he may get bread for his hungry guests. Prayer, Jesus implies, simply asks for what one needs, keeps knocking at the door that must be opened. It trusts the Father to be responsive to the asking child, more so than are earthly parents. "As bad as you are, you know how to give good things to your children" (verse 13). The Father can go further and do more: He can give the Holy Spirit to those who ask. The Holy Spirit is consistently portrayed as our prayer guide, our intercessor, the one who takes our needs and lays them before the Father, then takes the Father's resources and applies them to our needs. We do not need to find some special exotic place where we may pray. We need only practice the simplicity of prayer wherever we are. All we need is to know our need and to turn to Him who in prayer can meet it.

Lord, help me to understand the simplicity of prayer so I do not shut myself off from your blessings by creating my own complexities. Amen

Challenge: What problem in your life are you refraining from putting into God's hands because it is "too complex" for you to solve? Can you understand the ridiculousness of that and turn the whole complicated mess over to him?

Rocking-Chair Thoughts

"If I were hungry, I would not tell you, for the world and everything in it is mine" (Psalm 50:12).

"I'm rocking you, Grandpa."

Dr. Gerhard Frost—Sermon

To confuse our roles in this world is easy. One can enjoy visualizing Frost's granddaughter, delightedly giving herself to the rhythm of the rocking chair as she sits in his lap, and looking up into his face to announce "I'm rocking you." That was the way it seemed to her. Do we sometimes confuse our role with that of God? We make the church a busy place, organizing and publicizing, building and rebuilding, a constant bustle of socializing and banqueting. Then we can seem to say, "God, I'm rocking you."

We do this in our social lives, too—involving ourselves in good causes, rushing hither and yon, donating and financing—and seeing ourselves doing these things to advance the causes God favors. "God, I'm rocking you."

Do we do this even in our personal lives? We take good care of our adherence to proper moral standards; we are solid hard-working people obeying Paul's injunction to bear our own burdens. We go beyond that to care for our families and to help our neighbors. "God, I'm rocking you."

With all these things we do so well to support the work of God and his kingdom, it is rather shocking to read Psalm 50 and find God expressing such independence from our dutiful care of him and his cause. "... I do not need bulls from your farms nor goats from your flocks;.... If I were hungry, I would not tell you, for the world and everything in it is mine" (verses 9,12). Doesn't he appreciate all we have done? Frost is obviously delighted with his granddaughter's announcement "I'm rocking you." Doesn't God feel delight in our "rocking" him?

We smile at Frost's anecdote because we know better than the child, whose legs aren't even touching the floor. Eventually she will know that it was Grandfather's muscles that rocked her. God shows clearly in Psalm 50 that he wants us to realize that he is the source even of those things we think we are giving and doing for him.

Yet, having recognized that truth and given him his rightful sovereignty, we rejoice too in the fact that God has so tied his purposes on earth to our participation with him that there is a sense in which he "needs" our grateful service. But the power and the glory are his. No matter how noble our intentions, we are not "rocking" God.

Lord, help me to remember that all my life is a grateful and loving response to the way your strong arms support and surround me. I long for your saving help to be my sufficiency. Amen.

Challenge: Examine the good works you are involved in. Do you find any evidence that you have been doing them to "rock" God?

The Mother Love of Our Father

"It was you who brought me safely through birth, and when I was a baby, you kept me safe" (verse 9).

"But when such love exists between a poor pioneer woman and her plain, ordinary children, what must it not be when it rises to Divinity. . . ." The love of mother and child can be only an infinitesimal part of that other love; yet, small and imperfect as it is, it still carries a breath of the Divine omnipotence. . . . If you, pioneer mothers, have not seen the Glory of the Lord, then no preacher of the gospel will ever be able to show it to you!"

O.E. Rolvaag, <u>Giants in the Earth</u>

The itinerant pastor in *Giants in the Earth*, seeks to bring comfort and healing to the troubled immigrant woman, Beret. In his sermon in Per Hansa's' sod house, he draws an analogy between the love of the pioneer mother for her children and the love of God for his people. God is a spirit, so the only reason for a masculine pronoun for him is that the neuter seems inappropriate in our ignorance of spirit being. But if, as I believe we may assume, both the masculine and feminine are present in the nature of God who created us, we may truly use the analogy of the father-care and the mother-love which he extends to us. Troubled as the love of Beret is for her children, "it still carries a breath of the Divine Omnipotence." Other of her faculties have left her as her personality fragments, but the love for her child is there, anxious and enduring. The pastor senses the God-origin of that love. "If you, pioneer mothers, have not seen the glory of the Lord then no preacher of the gospel will ever be able to show it to you."

Psalm 122 is a Messianic psalm, one of those in which we hear the voice of the Son in the agony of his crucifixion pleading for the presence and rescue of the Father. "It was you," he prays, "who brought me safely through birth"—in a manger at the end of a dreary journey. "And when I was a baby, you kept me safe"— from the soldiers of Herod and on the long journey to Egypt. Love followed him—the love of the God-Father and human Joseph; the love of the God-Mother and the human mother, Mary. There was the fullness of the love of God, beyond our ability to fully comprehend, and the beauty of the most admirable of human love from Mary and the no-doubt-amazed Joseph, trying to understand what his marriage to Mary had brought into his life.

"I have relied on you since the day I was born, and you have always been my God," the psalmist says. That reliance and constancy give to life the experience of love that can make of it a great experience, whether we refer to the love and care of a devoted mother such as Mary was, or to the "steadfast love of the Lord." His constancy surpasses even hers. In that love, we experience the support and nourishment that leads us to victory in an unsteady and often frightening world.

Lord, "I have relied on you since the day I was born, and you have always been my God,...(verse 10). People not yet born will be told: 'The Lord saved his people.'" Praise you! Amen. (verse 31).

Challenge: Who in your relationship gives evidence of special need of a really supportive and nourishing love? Pray that God may direct that love through you to the one who needs it.

Being Part of the Body

"Let us not give up the habit of meeting together, as some are doing" (verse 25).

"To be of no church is dangerous. Religion, of which the rewards are distant, and which is animated only by faith and hope, will glide by degrees out of the mind unless it is invigorated and reimpressed by external ordinances, by stated calls to worship, and the salutory influence of example."
Samuel Johnson, <u>Lives of the Poets</u> *(Life of Milton)*

No doubt there have been times in the lives of all of us, as there have been in mine, when we have been ready to give up on the institutional church, and times when we have looked at what happened at church only to say, "Again, nothing happened that would make a difference in our lives. Just more reinforcement of a status quo that needs to be upset." Some of us get impatient with local congregations that seem insensitive to all needs except their own. Others are angry with denominational leaders whose positions are more liberal than their own—and others impatient with denominations which never prod their congregations to keener vision or more radical discipleship. Some are relieved when the demands that the church be more relevant to social needs seem to have died away. We are experts in suggesting ways the church would be better if only our ideas were followed.

No doubt Samuel Johnson saw much in the formalistic eighteenth century Church of England he would have liked to change. But he was a thinker and an observer, which led him to realize the necessity of the church in the life of the believer. He knew enough of human nature to know how easily our Christian faith and practice are eroded if that which is abstract and internal is not reinforced by what is concrete and external.

To be a Christian is not only to be an individual believer; it is to be a part of a body. It is not only to be a member of a body of believers, but also to have been granted by grace an individual relationship with the God who has established the body. Both aspects are vital.

Many of us who have grown up with the Bible camp experience have stood around campfires and watched as someone has separated one log from the fire, only to observe how it has smouldered and turned black. Spiritually the same thing has happened to many who have supposed they could safely separate themselves from the church, that body in which the fire of the Holy Spirit might be allowed to glow, to create the warmth of fellowship and the energy of love.

It was fascinating in the 1960s, at a time when youth seemed to be finding "the church" irrelevant in increasing numbers, the "Jesus movement" grew among youth and drew attention. Many churches retooled their youth programs to provide opportunity for young Christians who found the church indeed relevant and a setting for their enthusiastic witness. We were reminded of One who said, "I will build my church."

Thank you for what the congregations to which I have belonged have meant in stabilizing and maintaining my spiritual life, in bringing to me your saving help, O Lord. Amen.

Challenge: What are the most commonly heard complaints against your church? Take time to formulate in your mind, ready for use, as honest a defense as you can against that criticism. Then use it.

Both...And

"You are also God's building" (verse 9).

"The Lord showed me, so that I did see clearly, that he did not dwell in these temples which men had commanded and set up, but in people's hearts . . . and his people were his temple, and he dwells in them."
George Fox, *Journal* [1684]

Man's ideas of where he is to meet with God and worship him have changed down through the centuries. Jacob dreams of God's blessing, wakens, erects a stone monument to mark the place, and names it Bethel, the House of God. In the wilderness, there is the Tent of Meeting, outside the camp, where from the pillar of cloud God speaks and the people bow low. In spite of standing stones being forbidden as representations of God (Lev. 26:1), a pillar of such stones is erected when the Hebrews cross into the promised land (Josh. 4:19-24)—the stones as a reminder, not an object of worship.

When they come into the land, there is to be only one place of worship, Moses tells them: "...the Lord will choose the one place where the people are to come into his presence and worship him" (Deut. 12:5). While earlier the sacrifices had been part of worship in the movable tabernacle, later they will be in Jerusalem, at the temple built by Solomon. To Solomon, this is almost too great to believe. "But can you, O God, really live on earth? Not even all of heaven is large enough.... Watch over this temple day and night, this place where you have chosen to be worshipped" (I Kings 8:27-29). In that temple God's people are to worship. After the temple was destroyed, the synagogue and the home became centers of worship. This practice continues today, al-

9

though no place will mean fully what the temple did in Jewish worship.

George Fox, saintly leader of the English Quakers, for whom worship was a quiet seeking for the Inner Light, did not find the presence of God in the majestic cathedrals in his land. He was convinced that the Lord had shown him clearly that not in cathedrals but in the hearts of his people did God reveal himself and come to dwell.

How shall we understand the contradictions? Where shall we find him? The God who seeks in mercy and with grace the allegiance of our hearts does not reveal himself only in dreams on a stony pillow, or in the wilderness tabernacle, in majestic temples, or in the solitude of the individual. Wherever we turn to him in penitence and worship, he is near, and there we may listen for his words to us.

Thank you, great God of all, that you will meet me and accept my worship in every kind of setting in which I seek you out. Amen.

Challenge: Experiment with at least three different kinds of settings—e.g., your own bedroom, a quiet outdoor retreat, the hush of the sanctuary in your church—to see which for you is most conducive to a spirit of worship and prayer. (The effectiveness of these settings may vary with your moods and needs.) Perhaps you will sense the presence of God in all three.

Bigger Spoons

"They also learn to waste their time in going around from house to house..." (verse 13).

"I have measured out my life in coffee spoons."
T. S. Eliot, "The Love Song of J. Alfred Prufrock"

Eliot's character Prufrock finds life so dull because he has neither a sense of self-worth nor a purpose in life. Off to another coffee party, though unsure if he will have courage to go in where people may comment on his bald spot or think his words foolish, he knows his own emptiness. He knows he will feel like an insect pinned against the wall. His world is so insecure that he feels his every move disturbs the universe. He knows he has measured out his life in those tiny spoons that grace the tables of the parties he attends.

Paul in our Scripture verse is concerned that the people of the church at Thessalonica not measure out their lives in coffee spoons. The "going around from house to house" provides the training ground for learning to be "gossips and busybodies talking of things they should not." Today "Dear Abby" gets complaints that someone cannot get her work done because her neighbor comes too often and for too long. Men have their counterparts of the same kind of situation.

All of us occasionally need to do an "efficiency check" on the way we spend our time. I have found myself settling into ruts in which I spend hours in useless repetitive activities. We don't disturb the universe half as much as we expect when we withdraw from empty routines.

We need the fellowship and company of others. There are many ways of enjoying them aside from pinning others, insect-like, to our walls, or "going around from house to house," learning to be gossips and busy-bodies. How about reading a good book and discussing it with a group of our friends? Or watching a good documentary on television and sharing our ideas about its subject? Or reading our church paper together with friends? Or putting our family history in writing for our grandchildren or nieces and nephews?

Prufrock imagines himself finding satisfaction with mermaids under the sea, but it does not work. Even in his imagination he drowns. We can use our imaginations to plan creative ways of being with others in which we can both be blessed and be a blessing.

Lord, I long for your saving help to keep me from measuring out my life in coffee spoons. May I spend my life for something that will outlast it. In Jesus' name. Amen.

Challenge: Read John 1-12, watching how Jesus uses his times of being with others creatively. Think how you in your life situation could adapt his techniques in your own life.

A Hunger for Seriousness

"...whoever drinks the water that I will give him will never be thirsty again" (verse 14).

"...someone will forever be surprising
A hunger in himself to be more serious,..."
                    Philip Larkin, "Church Going"

A cyclist, in Larkin's poem, having checked to make sure a church is empty, steps within and lets the door thud shut behind him. The musty silence prompts him to remove his cycle-clips. He mounts the lectern and with a kind of bravado rehearses a "Here ends..." from the open book on the lectern, startling himself with the sound of his own voice. Back at the door he signs the guest-register, drops an Irish sixpence in the box, and stops before leaving to muse, as he evidently has before, what use this building and others like it eventually will be put to. Will some come to be museums? Architectural exhibits? Interesting ruins—like many of the post-Reformation abbeys in England? "Who," he ponders, "will be those last to come to them because of their holy history, their nourishment of the human spirit in sacred solitude?" Something about the holy silence attracts him. Someone, he thinks, will always be stopping in. The purpose the building serves will never be obsolete, "Since someone will forever be surprising a hunger in himself to be more serious," and will gravitate to this consecrated ground.

How sad that so many churches today stand locked because of the danger of vandals, quenching the impulse of those who go by to step inside and breathe that holy silence. Something about an architecturally impressive church stills the heart and lifts the eyes. Being alone and quiet within a sanctuary is an experience that can lead one to "forever be surprising/A hunger in himself to be more serious."

In my high-school teaching days I chaperoned a class of high school seniors on their spring trip to Winnipeg. Our schedule included (at my suggestion) a visit to the St. Boniface Cathedral in Winnipeg's neighboring city. How would my small-town Protestant young people behave in a cathedral? I wondered. Would they be properly quiet if people were there to pray, or would they be their usual boisterous selves? I needn't have worried. There was only reverent stillness. They knew instinctively that such a place called for stillness, not only of the vocal cords but of the heart.

One of the most uplifting experiences I have known within "my" church came during a Lenten season when we maintained a twenty-four-hour prayer vigil at the altar, coming by ones or twos to kneel, or perhaps to read a devotional book left handily available. If more of us would quietly absorb the peace, would listen for the Voice in silence in our churches, we would not need to wonder what churches may someday be turned into. As Larkin knows, "Someone will forever be surprising a hunger in himself to be more serious."

Lord, you who have promised that you will build your church, we long for your saving help to tune our ears to hear your voice in the buildings in which your church gathers. Amen.

Challenge: Ponder I Kings 8 to discover what Solomon expected the temple he had built to do for his people spiritually.

My Green Trash Bag

"There is no one who is righteous, no one who is wise or who worships God" (verses 10-11).

"There is no man so good, who, were he to submit all his thoughts and actions to the laws, would not deserve hanging ten times in his life."
Michel de Montaigne
"On the Art of Conversation," <u>Essays</u>

My pastor did it again! He gave us a visual image that can go with us through the days beyond this week. We should imagine, he suggested, as we come to the communion table, that we lugged with us one of those big green trash bags, full of all those things in our lives we'd like to be rid of. And as we knelt to receive the bread and wine we could pitch that bag of trash over the railing and return to our pews leaving it behind. My mind fastened on that image, and since then I have been filling my personal trash bag. (I know myself well enough to recognize that my need for forgiveness is not limited to communion Sunday!) The author of Romans knew that, as did the sophisticated essayist, Montaigne.

What is going into my trash bag? Quite a potpourri! I hadn't left the church this morning before I had a variety of contributions to that bag. I was reminded of the counsel of C. S. Lewis' Screwtape, that senior devil who is uncle to a junior tempter named Wormwood, who has been assigned to win a new believer away from his Christian commitment. Always, Screwtape urges, keep the young man aware of the faults of other believers. Make him even resentful of having to kneel at the same altar rail as those with whom he would scorn to associate in weekday life.

Once in a while I find myself with some such attitudes. Screwtape would certainly approve.

Then there is the hymn that talks about shouting the hope that fills us. I might rationalize by saying that I am not the shouting type, but while I sing the hymn with others, it's been a long time since I've spoken much about the hope that fills us even in the hours right after church. Why, I might make someone uncomfortable! Right? Someone has said that many Christians are like the rivers emptying into the Arctic. They are frozen at the mouth. My shyness about witnessing to his glory and works belongs in that trash bag....

—right along with that self-centeredness that I am powerless to keep eradicated. Self-this and self-that: self-satisfaction, self-pity, self-doubt, self-praise. "I" trouble—a chronic disease. Let others do what needs to be done—I'm tired. Let someone else feed the hungry. I'll feed my bank account. Or perhaps, let me give a dollar or two, but don't ask me to give myself. Self-justification; self-defense. There isn't much room left in my big green bag after some more self is stuffed in. That self grows like a weed. And it's heavy. But over the railing it goes, as I hear "the body of Christ, given for you," and "the blood of Christ, shed for you." Back to my pew, I'm walking more lightly. "Let us thank God for his priceless gift" (II Cor. 9:15).

I long for your saving help, and I do thank you, O God, for the priceless gift of forgiveness. Amen.

Challenge: Make your own list of the three contributions to your personal trash bag which you would make with the greatest sense of relief. Leave them behind in prayer.

The Two Options

"But the heavens and the earth that now exist are being preserved by the same command of God, in order to be destroyed by fire" (verse 7).

*"Some say the world will end in fire,
Some say in ice."*
                    Robert Frost, "Fire and Ice"

We live in a day of much speculation about the future of the earth. Futurists suggest how we should plan for it. Premillenialists expect at any moment to be snatched up from it, leaving others to judgment. Many of us watch the increasing moral and economic stress of our time with the conviction that the human race will soon bring about its own extinction.

Robert Frost consolidates the theories of escatology into two: a fiery eruption, or the return of an ice age. He knows the prophecies of a great nuclear cataclysm, including, no doubt, that of our Bible passage. He has also heard the scientists speak of changes in Earth's temperatures, making human life impossible in the return of an ice age.

Fire and ice can be taken literally as means to Earth's end, but Frost, in the fashion of poets, gives them metaphysical meaning. He equates fire with desire—passion, greed, and puts it first among agents of destruction. He equates ice with hatred—what can chill an atmosphere faster than hate?—and recognizes in it another force strong enough to shatter civilization. It would suffice.

Greed and hatred are powerful forces in human society. If we are honest, we will admit they are powerful forces in us as individuals too. Murder—deliberate and unpremeditated—results when they are yielded to, as do quarrelsomeness and rape and theft. Part of our "loss of innocence" as children or young people occurs when we sense how powerful and destructive these forces can be within us or those we love.

The destruction of Earth by fire or ice would shock but probably not surprise us. How comforting to know that the in-dwelling power of God in our lives can garrison us against the evil effects of passion and hate and keep us safe to the day when we experience a new heaven and a new earth.

Our Father, you who know the evils that threaten to dominate us, we long for your saving help to keep control over them in our individual beings and in our society. In your power and love. Amen.

Challenge: Search your own attitudes to make sure no hidden anger is building into passion or hatred.

Inescapable Associations

"Your enemy, the Devil, roams around like a roaring lion, looking for someone to devour" (verse 8).

Goodman: "We are a people of prayer, and good works to boot, and abide no such wickedness."
The traveler with the twisted staff: "Wickedness or not, I have a very general acquaintance here in New England. The deacons of many a church have drunk the communion wine with me; the selectmen of divers towns make me their chairman;…the governor and I, too—but these are state secrets."
Nathaniel Hawthorne
"Young Goodman Brown"

New Testament imagery for portraying the devil suggests both the roaring lion looking for prey and the angel whose brightness is a disguise to cover the evil form beneath. Modern imagery suggesting a cartoon character with a fork and a tail is far less effective, and suggests an unfortunate tendency to see evil as humorous, not to be taken seriously. There is much strange theology about the devil, even among some Christians, who seem to believe he is coequal with God and to be blamed for everything for which we humans do not want to take responsibility. Certainly it would be convenient to provide for those responsible for Auschwitz or lynch mobs—or ourselves—the excuse that "the devil made me do it."

Nathaniel Hawthorne, living in the early nineteenth century period called the Enlightenment, when many believed that the evils that plagued humankind would soon be overcome and that humans were moving closer to perfection, did not agree with that belief. He believed evil was a reality that had always plagued humanity, and the doctrine of human perfectibility was a dangerous deceit. In his "Young Goodman Brown," Goodman refuses to recognize his spiritual kinship with a sinning humanity. In his self-righteousness he sets himself up as judge and dies without comfort, no longer able to hear the word of grace.

Goodman believes that his ancestors have been different from those with a bent toward unrighteousness, that his pastor and deacon and fellow church people are "people of prayer and good works and abide no such wickedness." In the forest, that symbol of moral darkness, with his demonic guide, he is progressively disillusioned to find his father and grandfather, his pastor and deacon and Sunday School teacher are fellow-travelers with evil, and he goes home believing only himself to be uncorrupted.

The salvation that comes through grace comes only to those who admit their part in a humanity whose redemption required the death of God's own Son. We cannot, like Goodman, pride ourselves on being the holy exceptions, the ones who do not need forgiveness and grace. My identification with a fallen humanity in need of mercy not only puts me in a position in which mercy can redeem me, but puts me in a position in which I cannot self-righteously condemn others. The need they have for the grace of God is my need, too.

God of grace and mercy, I long for your saving help to know my need, which can cause me to rejoice in your gift of forgiveness through Jesus Christ. Amen.

Challenge: Take a few minutes for self-examination to see if in any corner of your thoughts you are basing your goodness on yourself or your associations rather than on Christ.

A World Grown Strange

"But whoever looks closely into the perfect law that
sets men free, who keeps on paying attention to it and
does not simply listen and then forget it, but puts it
into practice—that person will be blessed by God in
what he does" (verse 25).

"The world is all grown strange.
...How shall a man judge what to do in such times?
"As he has ever judged," said Aragorn. "Good
and ill have not changed since yesteryear; nor are they
one thing among Elves and Dwarves and another
among men. It is a man's part to discern them, as
much in the Golden Wood as in his own house."

J.R.R. Tolkien
<u>*Lord of the Rings: The Two Towers*</u>

There are times when I would like to say with
Eomer, "The world is grown strange," when I find
myself as puzzled as he about how a person shall judge
what to do in such times. Ordinary persons, whether
they be from America or from Middle-Earth, often today feel as if the values and the disciplines by which we
live have gone topsy-turvy. The values of many of the
television programs on my screen and the movies that
come to our town are not mine. My love of reading is
not enough to reconcile me to the kind of trash that fills
the counters at many bookstores. I don't find drunken-
ness humorous, disrespect for law cool, vandalism simply a form of youthful self-expression, or violence an
exhibition of macho. Bluntly stated, I sometimes don't
feel at home in this society at all. Nor do I believe in our
arming the world as millions starve.

I agree with Aragorn, the king to come, that while our understanding of what good and evil are may grow more sophisticated, "Good and ill have not changed since yesteryear," and it is a human's part to discern them. On the surface, the definition of evil in my home town in my childhood included such items as movies and folk dancing. Goodness often meant going faithfully through the old dull routines. But under those superficial surfaces, evil was what degraded and dehumanized; good was what affirmed and strengthened and brought forth love. A question useful now and then has to do with the effect of an act on the closeness of our relationship with God. Our time spent in arguments and rationalizings to defend our "right" to do the dubious are seldom well spent. There are more important matters—like love and supportiveness and generosity.

Feeling at home in a society in which standards seem to be crumbling leaves one full of tension. Yet there was One in a society that in his day seemed to be crumbling who made himself at home among tax-collectors and prostitutes, among zealots and thieves. Surely he had looked "closely into the perfect law that sets men free" and "put it into practice." Even if "the world is all grown strange" we can discern the goodness behind that perfect law that sets men free, rejoice in it, and let love be the motivation for behavior that affirms us as God's sons and daughters.

Lord, in a world where more and more I feel somewhat estranged, I long for your saving help to recognize that you have come to tabernacle among us. Amen.

Challenge: Compare your youthful criteria for separating wrong from right from those you use now. Are they more or less guided by love for God? Others? Your own well-being now?

The Widening Gyre

"Remember that there will be difficult times in the last days. People will be...violent" (verses 1, 3).

"Things fall apart; the center cannot hold;...
Mere anarchy is loosed upon the world,..."

W. B. *Yeats*
"The Second Coming"

The great Irish poet Yeats looked at the world of his day and did not like what he saw. Though not an orthodox Christian, he had his own theory of world history, one which saw time divided into periods approximately two thousand years in length, with each change of era marked by a great influential, cataclysmic event, such as the advent of Christianity in 4 B.C. Living in the early twentieth century, only a century away from the next change of era, Yeats saw a world falling apart before a "blood-dimmed tide" of violence and anarchy, a world in which good people did nothing, and evil people acted with passionate conviction. There seemed to be no center holding civilization together. Yeats wondered what great beast was "slouching toward Bethlehem" (the place of beginning) for the new era.

Yeats sees an analogy between a hunter having difficulty controlling his falcon (hunting hawk) and the world he knows. The falcon flown by his handler can readily be controlled if the gyre, the circle within which the cord tied to his leg confines him, is kept narrow. Then he can hear the master's voice. But if the gyre is allowed to widen so the falcon gets beyond the hearing of the handler, "things fall apart; the center cannot hold,..."

Paul writes to Timothy about "difficult times in the last days." He, too, envisioned a day in which "things fall apart," and "anarchy is loosed upon the world." Who of us in this day has not wondered if whatever center welds our society together will hold in the face of national and international turmoil, of violence on our streets, of a time in which many fortify their world with Saturday-night specials, more locks, and guard dogs. Desperate revolutionary forces born out of poverty, racism and injustice threaten to loose anarchy upon many lands, while the "best" imagine the answer to be the selling of weapons until the world is armed to the teeth.

Perhaps the "Second Coming" is what will soon occur. But whether it does or not, we need to keep within range of our Handler's voice, learning from him to "hunt" souls for his Kingdom with as great and fervent intensity as is evident in those on the side of evil.

We long for your saving help, O Lord, to live responsibly, so that your plan for the future may be fulfilled, and your Kingdom come. Amen.

Challenge: Reread II Timothy 3:1-5. Which of the kinds of behavior warned against do you see as most dangerous in your community? What are you doing about them?

A Higher Perspective

*"How clearly the sky reveals God's glory!
How plainly it shows what he has done!" (verse 1).*

*"At this latitude I'm spinning 836 miles an hour
round the earth's axis;...In orbit around the sun I'm
moving 64,800 miles an hour. The solar system as a
whole, like a merry-go-round unhinged, spins, bobs,
and blinks at the speed of 43,200 miles an hour along
a course set east of Hercules. Someone has piped, and
we are dancing a tarantella until the sweat pours....I
close my eyes and I see stars, deep stars giving way to
deeper stars, deeper stars bowing to deepest stars at
the crown of an infinite cone."*

Annie Dillard
<u>Pilgrim at Tinker Creek</u>

I had imagined myself, that day when I sat enjoying *Pilgrim at Tinker Creek,* to be spending a quiet day. All of a sudden I was almost dizzy, the effect of reading the sentences above. Quiet day, indeed! At 64,800 miles an hour, I might as well have called the spectacular telecasts of the rings of Saturn boring. Or have said of the appearance of a bacillus under a powerful microscope, "I've seen that before."

Perhaps it was the vastness of the desert sky that made the Biblical poets so aware of the heavens above them. Job faces question after question about the impenetrable stretches of space. "Do you know where the light comes from or what the source of darkness is?" (38:19). "Have you been to the place where the sun comes up, or the place from where the east wind blows?" (38:24). "Can you guide the stars season by season and direct the Big and Little Dipper? Do you know the laws that govern the skies, and can you make them apply to the earth?" (38:32-33).

Couched in the ancient cosmology that still influences our saying "The sun is going down," the poet's description of our sun declares "God made a home in the sky for the sun," and has it, like Apollo in his chariot, running the race from one end of the sky to the other (Ps. 19:4-5). Surely, "How clearly the sky reveals God's glory! How plainly it shows what he has done!"

Yet in the midst of all this whirl of cosmic activity, I may sit quietly aware of no more movement than that of the wind in the branches of the elm outside my window, or of the pen in my hand. "Someone has piped, and we are dancing a tarantella until the sweat pours," yes; but he has so marvelously balanced the movement that the gravity and motion so completely ordered can still leave me with a sense of perfect calm and quiet.

Those who can believe that all these phenomena resulted from the activity of the god Chance must have a great capacity for blind faith. Of the infinite intelligent plan which, rather than chance, brought all this marvel into being, we say, "Each day announces it [the glory of God] to the following day; each night repeats it to the next" (19:2).

Great Creator Lord, give me ears to hear the voice that goes out to all the world from your creation. Amen.

Challenge: Check out a book on astronomy from your public library and browse in it long enough to come to a fresh understanding of the vastness of space. It's all God's!

The Creator Had a Plan

"I am the one who created you.
I am the Lord, the Creator of all things.
I alone stretched out the heavens; when I made the
earth, no one helped me" (verse 24).

"For that without organization life does not exist is
obvious. Yet this organization itself is not strictly the
product of life, nor of selection. Like some dark and
passing shadow within matter, it cups out the eyes'
small windows or spaces the notes of a meadowlark's
song in the interior of a mottled egg."

Loren Eiseley
<u>The Immense Journey</u>

The argument between organic evolution and special creation has long gone on in religious and educa-
tional circles. Our own day is not the first in which this
matter of faith has been handed to the civil courts. To
reduce the issue to its most basic terms, we should
speak of the origin of the universe being the result
either of Chance or of the action of a Creator God. God
has revealed neither his method nor the length of time it
took him, though his defenders have proposed many
theories.

Arguments are most effective when they state the
issue in its basic terms. To argue whether life is a result
of, in James Weldon Johnson's imagery, a God who "sat
down on the hillside and thought and thought till he
thought 'I'll make me a man,'" or of progressive evolution is to evade the central issue. Who or what is behind
it all? The unbeliever says Chance. The question for the
believer is settled: the God who says "I am the one who
created you."

Biblical writers are consistent in their assumption that God is Creator/Lord. They never stop to argue the question. They know their beliefs are not universal: they know of peoples who worship spirits that inhabit wood and stone. They have some trouble coming to understand that their God is the God of the universe rather than their private possession. But this God speaks with authority: "I alone stretched out the heavens; when I made the earth no one helped me." His power is not diminished: "With a word of command I dry up the ocean."

The naturalist/poet/philosopher Loren Eiseley in the quotation above marvels at the plan and the predictable orderliness of the world to which his studies have led him. The meadowlark's song will not be a matter of chance, nor will this year's hatch of lovely singers on prairie fence posts sing a different song from that of last year. Already in the white of the bird's egg is the pattern. I find it hard to tell whether Eiseley would attribute this marvelous orderliness to Chance or to a God whose creativity and artistry are beyond our description. But I know that I find it impossible to believe that such marvelous design could come from undirected Chance. More blind faith is needed to believe in a world created by chance than to believe the design originated with a Creator God whose ways are far beyond our understanding.

Thank you, Lord God, for sharing the results of your artistry with me—and creating me as wonderfully as you did the meadowlark. Amen.

Challenge: What living thing aside from humans best evidences for you the creative artistry of God? Learn all you can about that species and use it as evidence to remind others of the marvels of God's creation.

Weeding Out The Baobabs

*"One night, when everyone was asleep, an enemy
came and sowed weeds among the wheat and went
away" (verse 25).*

*"Now there were some terrible seeds on the
planet that was the home of the little prince; and these
were the seeds of the baobab. The soil of that planet
was infested with them. A baobab is something you
will never, never be able to get rid of if you attend to it
too late....It's a question of discipline.... When you've
finished your own toilet in the morning, then it's time
to attend to the toilet of your planet. You must see to
it that you pull up regularly all the baobabs,..."*

Saint-Exupery
<u>The Little Prince</u>

Just as an unexpected lovely flower sometimes
grows out of a weed patch, so a beautiful work of
literature may grow out of a period of war and destruction. One evidence of this is Saint-Exupery's short classic, *The Little Prince*, a fantasy that came from occupied
France in World War II. The story can be meaningful
and rich in theme even for those who never think to
connect it with that war, but those who know its back-
ground recognize the "terrible seeds" that produce the
baobabs as Nazism, and know of the author's role in the
French underground. A pilot, he died in the crash of his
military plane in North Africa.

For most readers, the "terrible seeds" that infect
the soil of the little prince's planet, the baobabs, are
human evil. The baobab, an African tree that looks for
all the world like a deciduous tree with its roots in the
air, is a rapid-growth tree that works well as Saint-

Exupery's symbol of evil. Like evil, if allowed to get a start it grows exuberantly. Like Nazism, it becomes strong and unassailable before anyone rallies against it.

Christians, with their faith in God and in the ultimate victory of good over evil, sometimes find it easy to forget that "It's a question of discipline....You must see to it that you pull up all the baobabs." The "toilet of your planet" involves keeping evil from infecting the institutions of society as well as our own surroundings. It is popular in our day to be very tolerant of "baobabs" favored by others. The banners of the Moral Majority are soon matched by those of the Immoral Minority who object to the identification of their practices or pleasures as evil.

There are problems of individual freedom involved in our attack on some issues. We can pull up rose bushes in the process of uprooting baobabs. Probably we do most good in directing our attacks on those evils that are generally agreed on. Identifying a vote on the control of the Panama Canal as a baobab may meet honest disagreement. Few can seriously disagree that crime and apathy, war and plunder, bigotry and rape are baobabs that merit our attention and uprooting. The baobabs destroyed while still tiny plants will never produce the heartache of those that ignorance and laziness permit to become trees.

I long for your saving help, O Lord, to give me eyes to see the spiritual baobabs in my own yard, and courage to uproot them. Amen.

Challenge: What 'baobab' is the most destructive in the community in which you live? Who else in your community would be willing to join you in some specific resistance to its growth?

Successful in Vain

"I have complete confidence in the gospel;..." (verse 16).

"All we do know, and that to a large extent by experience, is that evil labours with vast power and perpetual success—in vain: preparing always only the soil for unexpected good to sprout in it. So it is in general, and it is so in our own lives."
The Letters of J. R. R. Tolkien

Tolkien's *The Lord of the Rings* is a fantasy depicting good and evil—a fantasy in which evil (Sauron) always seems to have the power and the success on his side, but good has greater invisible resources and wins at the last. The defenders of good seem small and slightly comic in the face of orcs and goblins and the Black Riders of Mordor. But these evil beings have unseen weaknesses—they are inevitably subject to the results of their own evil: they are jealous, disloyal, filled with hatred. They are contemptuous of the forces of good, unable to understand that in the hobbit Frodo, the wizard Gandalf, and king-to-be Aragorn, they are opposing the power of the One, who can use his suffering servant, his prophet, and his king to save Middle Earth for himself and his people.

Tolkien writes his letter to his soldier-son in World War II, both of them feeling the weight of evil rampant in their world. Out from the tale he has been weaving for years, the father draws for comfort the same theme of the ultimate triumph of good over that evil that "labours with vast power and perpetual successes—in vain." All it can do is "prepare the soil for unexpected good to sprout in." So it will be in the life of the Oxford don and in that of the young airman training in South Africa.

That takes faith, the kind of faith of one who can say "I have complete confidence in the Gospel" because the God who gave us the good news of the gospel is the ultimate conqueror of this world's evil. Evil may compile its list of successes—and they may be impressive. But they are also, we know by faith, in vain. Just as God used the perfidy of Joseph's brothers for eventual good ("It was really God who sent me ahead of you" Gen. 45:5), just as his hand was in Esther's being chosen the favorite queen of Xerxes' harem ("Yet who knows—maybe it was for a time like this that you were made queen!" Esther 4:14), so he will use our conflict with evil as the soil in which his ultimate victory will appear. We may be much more like the little hobbit than like the king or the prophet on God's side, but nevertheless we will share in that victory. And one of these times, we will find that the struggle is over for keeps, because our God has kept us with complete confidence in the gospel.

I long for your saving help, O Lord, not to become discouraged by the successes of evil but to know by faith that they are shallow and will ultimately crumble. Amen.

Challenge: Train yourself to respond to every announcement evil makes of its successes with "Your success is in vain. My God is a God of ultimate victory."

It's Your Fault, God

"The woman you put here with me gave me the fruit and I ate it" (verse 12).

> *"There are only two or three human stories, and they go on repeating themselves as fiercely as if they had never happened before."*
> Willa Cather, <u>O Pioneers</u>

We call myths those "human stories" that "go on repeating themselves" in the history of humankind. The details may change but they identify the same kind of action; they reveal human behavior in the same way. The story of temptation, disobedience, and the attempt to refuse responsibility that we find in Genesis 3 has gone on repeating itself in every society and every individual, and many times in a single life. With what marvelous succinctness the author tells the story!

Eve, tempted first to doubt God's words and then to question his intent, yields to persuasion and eats the fruit, then gives to her husband who, from what we are told, puts up little resistance. But judgment is not long in coming as God walks in the garden. "Did you eat the fruit that I told you not to eat?" Adam's answer is the very human precursor of millions of attempts to "pass the buck." Harry Truman may have said "The buck stops here," but Adam hurried to pass it on. "The woman you put here with me gave me the fruit and I ate it."

Did you notice where the buck landed? Not on Adam, but divided neatly between God and Eve. "The woman *you put here*—Now see what happened, God!" "*She* gave me the fruit." Now if you had only left things as they used to be before she came around…! But the excuses do not change the reality—"I ate it."

One of the most obvious inheritances Adam passed on to the human family is the desire to shift blame for failures and disobedience. In his marvelous imaginative description of what he thinks hell must be like, C. S. Lewis in *The Great Divorce* visualizes Napoleon pacing his room in hell, trying to cast from himself the responsibility for his defeat. "Josephine did it...Sault did it..." If he could have accepted the onus for his own mad decisions, perhaps the scene would not have been in hell.

It is so humbling to have to take the blame upon ourselves for what we do—especially when our acts illustrate the human story that goes on repeating itself as if it had never happened before. Only One has broken the chain of that repetition—and he cast no blame but prayed for forgiveness for others who were truly guilty. A better prayer than Adam's would be "These you have placed here with me have sinned—and I with them."

Lord, give us the humility to accept the blame for what we do. I long for your saving help to confess sin and claim your forgiveness. In Jesus' name. Amen.

Challenge: Reread Chapter 3 of Genesis watching the characters' reaction to guilt. Note how 3:15 has within itself the promise of salvation.

The Kiss of Death

"The man I kiss is the one you want. Arrest him!"
(verse 48).

"Yet each man kills the thing he loves,
By this let each be heard,
Some do it with a bitter look,
Some with a flattering word,
The coward does it with a kiss,
The brave man with a sword."
Oscar Wilde, "The Ballad of Reading Gaol"

Of all the Bible characters the hardest for me to understand is Judas. I find it impossible to believe that Judas responds to Jesus' invitation to be his disciple and travels with him on those dusty roads of Galilee and Judea without coming to love him. But whatever the motivation that leads him to become the traitor, Judas that evening "kills the thing he loves" and lives on in our memories in infamy.

Oscar Wilde in "The Ballad of Reading Gaol" has his persona, like Wilde a prisoner, caught in the tension of the prison one morning when a murderer, condemned for a crime of passion, is to be hanged. As he thinks of the condemned man, he cannot help but realize that the man who has been apprehended and condemned is really different from countless others only in degree. He has killed with an obvious weapon the woman he loved. The forces of justice have laws to deal with those who kill with knives. But Wilde's observer had enough moral sensitivity to know that the act of snuffing out life or the worth of living doesn't happen only by knives or swords, and that many who violate the lives of others are never condemned by society. The attack may be by bitter words, flattery, desertion, ridicule, pervertedly directed against those we love. Wilde included Judas too: "The coward does it with a kiss."

"The man I kiss is the one you want. Arrest him!" Judas could be brave with the soldiers at his back. But his bravery didn't last long, not when he realized that Jesus would use no miracle to defend himself, that whatever his motive he, Judas, had "killed the thing he loved." Neither Roman or Jewish justice would put Judas to death. His own self-condemnation would do that.

What strange combinations of love and hate our natures are! All of us know the bewildering flashes of hate or resentment striking out at someone we love— and the fact that we go unreproved makes us feel even worse. Only God's mercy can remedy the wrong, and only his grace can forgive the sin and bring us healing.

I long for your saving help, O Lord, to control my unpredictable emotions, so that nothing I say or do will kill "the thing I love." Amen.

Challenge: Reread the Joseph story with its account of how his brothers seek his death (Genesis 37).

Seeing Our Real Faces

"So I find that this law is at work: when I want to do what is good, what is evil is the only choice I have" (verse 21).

"The life of every man is a diary in which he means to write one story, and writes another; and his humblest hour is when he compares the volume as it is with what he vowed to make it."

> *James Matthew Barrie*
> *The Little Minister*

In C. S. Lewis' mythic novel *Till We Have Faces*, he creates the character of the Princess Orual who records the story of her life in order to show how unjust and unkind the gods have been to her. Though she wears a veil because she believes her face is ugly, she is confident of her moral righteousness and ready to assess fault in others. She condemns one sister as selfish and vain; the other she idolizes and claims to love dearly. The military leader of her army she monopolizes until his family seldom sees him; her Greek tutor she gives freedom too late for him to enjoy it. Finally, through a series of painful experiences, she can remove her veil and see herself not as the wronged victim of other people's neglect and dislike but as one who devours others, leaving her sisters lonely and misjudged, her general worn out and his wife resentful, and her tutor aware that what he has taught her has not helped her to find her own "face" (self-knowledge). At the last she must admit she has had little insight into her own motives and actions. Truly, as Barrie said, "The life of every person is a diary in which he means to write one story, and writes another." Orual has her humblest hour when she is forced to look at her real face.

The Apostle Paul knew the same struggle between what he wanted to be and what he really was. He had wished to be the Great Defender of the God of Abraham, Isaac and Jacob, but found himself the Great Persecutor of God in Christ. Even after his conversion he knew the universal contradiction between what we aspire to be and what we are. We are hurt and offended when others misjudge our actions or our integrity, but often we are forced to realize that our own assessment of our motives is dubious at best.

Many people in our day advocate the keeping of a spiritual diary or journal which helps us to see ourselves and our progress toward honesty and sanctification more accurately. Even in them, honesty of Paul's kind is difficult to attain—yet so necessary to our spiritual maturing.

Lord, I long for your saving help to give me the courage to look honestly at my motives and behavior, to dare to be honest about myself. Amen.

Challenge: Experiment with keeping a journal in which you record the account of your spiritual life. Do it long enough to be able to observe growth.

Tough Love

"Love must be completely sincere....Love one another warmly as Christian brothers, and be eager to show respect for one another" (verses 9-10).

"Love all God's creation, the whole and every grain of sand in it. Love every leaf, every ray of God's light. Love the animals, love the plants, love everything. If you love everything, you will perceive the divine mystery in things. Once you perceive it, you will begin to comprehend it better every day. And you will come at last to love the whole world with an all-embracing love."

Fyodor Dostoevsky
<u>*The Brothers Karamazov*</u>

There is a phrase one hears occasionally today which I find intriguing: tough love. Such love could have done the Karamazovs a great deal of good if they had practiced it. Too often we think of love as namby-pamby, soft and mushy, easy-going and yielding. "Tough love" names the philosophy of those who believe that a parent shows real love to a child when that love includes discipline, teaching, an explanation of boundaries, the willingness to say and enforce "No" as well as "Yes." Tough love means challenging someone to develop a sturdy backbone. It doesn't give in and abdicate the responsibility to set and uphold standards. Some people in our day confuse love with permissiveness, even in matters of religion. They say God doesn't really expect us to respect and obey the ancient guidance his law gives us. He knows we like to be popular and do what others favor. If we do as we like, his grace will cover our acts and forgive our sins. "Cheap grace"

Dietrich Bonhoffer called such a teaching—using grace lightly because it is plentiful and comes free.

Belief in cheap grace insults God's love. Love and grace come to us at a great cost to God, just as tough love comes to us at the cost of discomfort and pain on the part of the one who exercises it. Tough love often brings about results among young people who have not previously known boundaries enforced by parents or counselors. Wisely and firmly drawn boundaries are signs of love. Parents who ignore their responsibilities to provide them may think they are being liberal and generous to their children. I have often found that students who write about their relationships with their parents look at such "freedom" as a sign of lack of love and concern. "They didn't care" is often the interpretation. God does care about the quality of the life we live as his children. Yes, there is grace and mercy when we slip and fall. There is also the firm admonition that love is to be sincere, warm, and full of real respect for others. "Work hard and do not be lazy." "Serve the Lord with a heart full of devotion." "Share your belongings." "Open your house to strangers." We are not called upon to extend a mushy, sleezy love to others, but rather to demand of ourselves tough love that asks the best from others, but especially from ourselves.

Loving Lord, I long for your saving help to show tough and abiding love to others and to live respecting God's "tough love" for me. Amen.

Challenge: Examine carefully your own brand of love toward your family and friends. Is there some instance where you have been satisfied to show a sentimental kind of love where tough love is needed?

Too Dear a Price

"Keep away from evil! Refuse it and go on your way"
(verse 15).

"Wisdom, whose lessons have been represented
as so hard to learn by those who never were at her
school, only teaches us to extend a simple maxim
universally known. And this is, not to buy at too dear
a price."

Henry Fielding
The History of Tom Jones

All of us have had the experience of paying out good money for what we hoped was a wise purchase but what turned out to be embarrassingly worthless or even harmful. Grumpily we mutter to ourselves that next time we will remember the old saying that we get only as much as we pay for.

In Stephen Crane's story "The Blue Hotel," the Swede, convinced that in a Wild West town he is ringed with danger, goads a gambler into an angry response with his dagger. As the Swede lies dying, his eyes seem to be fastened on the legend of the cash register, "This registers the amount of your purchase."

"Wisdom," says Fielding, "teaches us…not to buy at too dear a price." Life is full of examples of poor buys. Perhaps some of the most effective examples are those we learn by observing the lives of others. Nothing but the grace of God can protect us from these poor purchases—and even then, scars are left which grace can use but not erase:

—the popularity that comes at the cost of giving up our convictions;

—the misuse of alcohol and narcotics that brings with it the end of self-respect and respect from others;

—the few minutes of lust that result in an unwanted human life that must endure for many decades;

—the chance to impress our associates with our superiority that loses us friends;

—the "thrill" of a suspenseful moment of shoplifting that leaves us horrified when we are caught and our coveting is plainly called thievery;

—the opportunity for a verbal thrust at someone in our family that leaves us sick inside for hours.

I once heard an anecdote about the little boy who had fun pounding nails into the fine oak of a door frame in his home. Apprehended by his father, who pointed out what damage had been done, the child pleaded with his father to undo the damage. The father pointed out that while he could forgive, he could not remove the marks that the hammer had left.

The grace of God surpasses knowledge and can even redeem scarred bodies and souls, but how much better to "Refuse evil and go on your way," to "keep away from evil" in the first place that we may not grieve him whose grace is sufficient. Check out the price before you buy!

I long for your saving help, O Lord, to know what is right and good that I may refrain from buying what goes into my life at too dear a price. Amen.

Challenge: Examine the life you have lived today to see if there is anything you have purchased at too high a cost.

The Beauty of Holiness

*"Do what I say, and you will live. Be as careful to
follow my teaching as you are to protect your eyes"
(verse 2).*

*I know a lady with a terrible tongue,...
All her perfections tarnished—and yet it is not long
Since she was lovelier than any of you."*
John Crowe Ransom, "Blue Girls"

Modern poets are seldom moralizers. If they deal
with moral advice it is usually in an indirect manner
that leaves the reader to intuit the lesson involved. One
of the poems in which the message is clear and direct is
John Crowe Ransom's "Blue Girls." The speaker is evidently walking by a girls' school at a time when the
girls with their blue uniforms are relaxing on the cam-
pus lawns. He notices their carefreeness, aware that
they will likely seem to listen to their teachers, "old and
contrary," and pay little heed. The future disturbs them
no more than it does the "birds that flit about on the
grass/and liven the air with their songs."

Even in the face of their carefreeness, the teacher in
him cannot resist a warning to them to cherish their
beauty. He promises to use his poetic art to "publish
beauty." The reason for his concern comes out in the
stanza above. He remembers one who had once been as
beautiful as the girls he is watching until her "terrible
tongue" and "blear eyes" reveal her deterioration.

Most of us who have lived long enough can verify
Ransom's example. We, too, have known someone once
beautiful who as time went on has developed a disposition turned sour, an expression grown hard, a reputation spoiled. Beauty, to be preserved, must be prac-

ticed, as must one's ability to play an instrument. The person who carefully uses the finest skin cream to maintain physical beauty often seems unaware that soul beauty needs just as much maintenance.

Ransom suggests that one of the destructive forces that corrupts personal beauty is a "terrible tongue." All of us know someone whose terrible tongue has ruined professional relationships with colleagues. Dare we say quickly, "That has nothing to do with me"? Who of us is free from memories of cutting speech gone out of control to savage someone we love—or someone who needed our tenderness.

And what about those "blear eyes"? Are they blood-shot with weeping over lost spiritual beauty? Lost physical beauty drained away to narcotics or alcohol or promiscuity?

The personalities shaped by God's Spirit grow more beautiful with the years and continue to do so, for God isn't done with us yet. When he is, we will have the beauty of his likeness.

Lord, I long for your saving help that I may worship you in the beauty of holiness. Amen.

Challenge: Spend at least as much time today in spiritual grooming as in grooming your physical appearance.

No Excuse at All

"Do you, my friend, pass judgement on others? You have no excuse at all, whoever you are" (verse 1).

"He stood appalled, judging himself with the thoroughness of God, while the action of mercy covered his pride like a flame and consumed it. He had never thought himself a great sinner before but he saw now that his true depravity had been hidden from him lest he despair....He saw that no sin was too monstrous for him to claim on his own, and since God loved in proportion as He forgave, he felt ready at that instant to enter Paradise."

Flannery O'Connor
"The Artificial Nigger"

Mr. Head, in Flannery O'Connor's story from which our quotation is taken, considers himself an upright man, one whom his young grandson would do well to imitate. But then comes that shocking experience when, on the streets of the frightening, unfamiliar city, the boy collides with a woman and her sack of groceries and upsets both, and Mr. Head in his embarrassment denies that he even knows the boy. The boy, frightened and horrified at his grandfather's denial of him, follows at a distance from then on and refuses to speak to him. Mr. Head's conscience brings home to him his depravity (like that of Peter denying his Lord), and for the first time he comes to understand sin and grace. It is when he judges himself "with the thoroughness of God" that the action of mercy can cover his pride and consume it. Rather than despairing, he comes to know that "God loved in proportion as He forgave," and there is much to forgive.

In a time when many seem hesitant to speak of personal guilt and of people being brought by the Holy Spirit under the conviction of sin, there are contemporary fiction writers who do not flinch from such subjects. The pious, self-righteous woman in the prison scene of Graham Greene's *The Power and the Glory* is far less likely to be the recipient of grace than is Greene's "whiskey priest" with his alcoholism and his mistress and his child. Flannery O'Connor's characters also must often be brought to an insight into their own hypocrisy before they can know grace.

The moral failure in these characters is often their judgmental attitude toward others, which accompanies unawareness of their own grotesque moral deformities. Is any sin more prevalent among believers than that of judgmental attitudes? Jesus and Paul, whose words set the pattern for Christian behavior, condemn the assumption of the right to judge others. It is not that we are to be blind to evil and wrongdoing. Some day, Paul tells the Corinthian Christians, they are going to judge the world (I Cor. 6:2). But that time is not yet, and until then, when full knowledge has replaced partial knowledge, "you have no excuse at all, whoever you are," for judging. The excuses we use are many. The reasons too often involve our assumption that because we see and judge wrong, we are superior to those in whom we identify it. That is not necessarily true.

Lord, I long for your saving help to deal with my judgmental attitudes and develop in me a more humble spirit, like yours. Amen.

Challenge: Keep an honest count for the next day or two of those times you find yourself judging someone else. How often can you keep yourself from giving in to that temptation?

The Use of Our Lips

"God's message is near you, on your lips and in your heart—that is, the message of faith that we preach" (verse 8).

(The doctor) "It's an odd thing about my body. Here I've lived in it all these years and how little use I've had of it. Now it's going to die and decay never having been used. I wonder why it did not get another tenant." He smiled sadly over this fancy but went on with it. "Well, I've had thoughts enough concerning people and I've had the use of these lips and a tongue but I've let them lie idle. When my Ellen was here living with me I let her think me cold and unfeeling while something within me was straining and straining trying to tear itself loose."

Sherwood Anderson, "Unlighted Lamps"

Sherwood Anderson's doctor in "Unlighted Lamps" has come to a moment of truth. His strong helping hands have shown his concern for his patients, but out in the evening his lonely daughter walks, wondering how she can break down the wall of silence between herself and her father. He had loved his wife, but finally she had left him, his love still unexpressed. Now, just before a coronary occurs, he resolves too late to open up and speak the love his daughter yearns for. The lamp of communication so much needed by both goes unlighted.

The doctor is not the only one among us to realize "I've had the use of these lips and a tongue but I've let them lie idle." Is not that for many of us what has happened with the good news of the gospel? It is indeed near us, on our lips and in our hearts, but we, like the doctor with his unspoken message of love, have let the message of grace lie idle.

Stop for a count. With how many people are you comfortable speaking about Christ and what his love and grace mean in your life? Three? Ten? Twenty? None? Perhaps twenty is the most comfortable number for many of us, for then we are speaking to a group rather than to an individual. We are part of Christ's body. Do we, too, say "Here I've been part of it all these years and how little use I've had of it"? How little— while I have spoken facilely of weather, politics, neighbors, television—I have said about God's message which is near me, the message of faith! How often, even in our closest circle of friends, would a venture to speak of what Christ means in our lives be met with embarrassment or silence?

We have all heard someone pose the question, "If you were brought before a court accused of being a Christian, would there be enough evidence to convict you?" How many hours of evidence would it take if the prosecuting attorney were listening to our words to find that evidence? Perhaps many of us are the type who speak least about the things that matter most to us. So it was with Anderson's doctor, whose most important words were never spoken because of that trait in his character. And so it may be with God's message which is on our lips and in our heart. It may never be spoken unless we go counter to our ourselves.

Lord, I long for your saving help to unfasten my speech and my inhibitions that I may be a better witness to you. Amen.

Challenge: Find an occasion this week to speak with someone close to you about what is happening in your spiritual growth and appreciation of what your faith means to you.

Scapegoat

"The goat will carry all their sins away with him into some uninhabited land" (verse 22).

"Christ of His gentleness
Thirsting and hungering,
Walked in the wilderness...
And ever with Him went...
Bleeding foot, burning throat,
The guileless old scapegoat;...

Robert Graves, "In The Wilderness"

The scapegoat was not sacrificed; that happened to the other of two goats. On the head of the scapegoat the priest symbolically placed the sins of the people and it was driven away into the wilderness. Even for a goat with its propensity for eating almost anything, the desert wilderness was a sparse, desolate place to live. Even goats like some companionship, and the wilderness offered little—unless in their wanderings the goats from the ceremonies of other years found each other. It shouldn't happen to a goat!

Graves imagines in his poignant poem that an exiled goat saw Jesus, recognized in him a kindred being, and followed him the entire forty-day stint, guarding him and sharing his trials. The scapegoat had been driven out of the settlement; Jesus, on the other hand, was led out by the Spirit. The goat was to be the symbolic atonement for Israel's sins; Jesus to atone for the sins of the world. Both of them were outside the city boundaries, away from the solace that others of one's kind can be. Both of them were there because of the sins of others rather than their own.

"For this reason Jesus also died outside the city, in order to purify the people from sin with his own blood. Let us, then, go to him outside the camp and share his shame" (Heb. 13:12-13). "Outside the camp" in Old Testament times was the place for the unclean, the diseased, the deserted. It was the place for those who were not ritually clean, for the lepers, for those who had touched dead bodies. "Outside the camp" was Golgatha, "the place of a skull." Our Lord was there. Handled and abused by Gentiles in Herod's court, he was ritually unclean. He offered himself for those afflicted with the leprosy of sin; he had touched dead bodies and restored them to life—and for that he was the scapegoat for those who, as he himself said, "knew not what they did."

"Outside the camp" was a place of thirst and hunger. But it was also a place of prayer, a place in which angels ministered to him, in which he grew strong by wrestling with temptation. That infinite kindness and gentleness, the poet imagines, even an old scapegoat could sense and desire to follow. It is in the taking our place with him outside the camp that something redemptive can develop in our lives and give us a ministry to share with him for others.

I long for your saving help, O Lord, to make me willing to share that place outside the camp with you that I may learn how to help lift the burdens from others. Amen.

Challenge: Who among your friends is struggling with a personal weakness of sin from which he or she needs release? What can you do to share the struggle and lift that weight from tired shoulders?

The Unshared Experience

If you confess that Jesus is Lord and believe that God raised him from the dead, you will be saved" (verse 9).

"The solid and unshared experience
Dies of itself...."

Archibald MacLeish,
"Speech to Those Who Say Comrade"

MacLeish in his poem speaks specifically of the comradeship between those who have shared the experience of war, who because of that seek each other out and have much in common to talk about—the battles, the grim moments of holding ground, the defeats, the welcome of those they came to liberate. These soldiers have shared experiences that were unforgettable, searing, future-shaping.

There is much of truth in MacLeish's words. We all know from experience, whether we have thought about it or not, that a way of clarifying and fixing an experience in our memories is to tell it to someone else. Only in such sorting out of the details as to make them clear to someone else do we see the implications of what we are saying.

Paul suggests a spiritual application of this truth. "If you openly admit by your mouth that Jesus Christ is the Lord, and if you believe in your own heart that God raised him from the dead, you will be saved."[1] The Bible knows nothing of the idea that our faith is a private matter between only God and us. As we learn to verbalize the truth that Jesus Christ is our Lord, we come to face the meaning of that in our daily lives. In that confession before others, we are challenged to make

---

[1]Romans 10:9-10, *The New Testament in Modern English*

our lives accord with our words. The risen Lord in whom we believe gives us the courage and the words by which we take our stand among God's people.

Do we find our verification of that if we listen to ourselves in our verbal exchange with others? We can seem to talk about everything else, private or public, but how frozen the stream of speech among even many church people if someone speaks a witness of what God is doing in his or her life experience! Some even seem embarrassed, as if what has been said is somewhat indelicate. We proudly admit to our friendships with other humans, but we are often so slow to let others know by our speech of our association with our Lord.

"If anyone declares publicly that he belongs to me," Jesus says, "I will do the same for him before my Father in heaven" (Matt. 10:32). We confess allegiance often in our lives. Paul says of the believer that "it is stating his belief by his own mouth that confirms his salvation."

Lord, forgive my silence about my faith in you. I long for your saving help, O Lord, that I may not be one of those whom you will disown because I have denied you in this life. Amen.

Challenge: Some time in the next twenty-four hours, begin (or continue) to build a habit of a daily verbal witness to your faith as you are prompted by the Holy Spirit.

Tumbling Down Walls

*"So there is no difference between Jews and Gentiles,
between slaves and free men, between men and
women; you are all one in union with Christ Jesus"
(verse 28).*

*"Something there is that doesn't love a wall,
That wants it down."*

Robert Frost, "Mending Wall"

The more one thinks of the implications of Paul's words to the Galatian Christians, the more amazing and revolutionary they become. The person who is comfortable only with the status quo would likely do best to go on to the next verse. For a Jew whose parents no doubt named him after the first Hebrew king, who could trace his lineage to the tribe of Benjamin, who was an eminent student of the great Gamaliel, who was a Pharisee—for him to say that the differences between Jew and Gentile have been done away in Christ and they are one, that was revolution!

Paul has often been criticized for not openly attacking slavery, that curse of the Roman world. To be a slave then often resulted from being one of a defeated people. A slave might be as educated or refined as his master. Did Paul sense that the Christian faith would soon bring not only corrupt Rome but the slavery which supported it crashing down around them faster than would a bloody revolution of slaves? Paul sent Onesimus, a runaway slave, back to his master, Philemon, asking the master to receive the slave like a Christian brother. But that is not all.

Paul has also been criticized for statements in which he makes women seem inferiors—e.g., women are to be saved only by their child-bearing, which exempts a great many of them from salvation. It is perhaps hard for us who are centuries away from Paul's cultural setting to accept what he is trying to say to those of his recently pagan congregation. But Paul also says in unmistakably clear language that spiritually there is no difference "between men and women; you are all one in union with Christ Jesus."

Do we really hear that "all one"? There is an unnamed list that is included in "all one": the Roman and the barbarian, the scholar and the anti-intellectual, the conservative and the liberal, the well-mannered and the boor, the Chippewa and the Sioux, the beautiful and the plain, the wrinkled hag and the fashion model, the rich and the poor, the black and the brown. The implications are endless: we are all one in Christ Jesus. Now how do we put that into practice?

God of love, we long for your saving help to remember that you have made us all one in Christ Jesus. Help us to live that way. Amen.

Challenge: Which group of "outsiders" is hardest for you personally to approach in love and friendship? What in the next week can you do to tumble the wall between yourself and them?

Only More So

"Don't you know that your body is the temple of the
Holy Spirit, who lives in you...?" (verse 19).

"Every man is the builder of a temple, called his
body, to the god he worships, after a style purely his
own, nor can he get off by hammering marble instead.
We are all sculptors and painters, and our material is
our own flesh and blood and bones. Any nobleness
begins at once to refine a man's features, any mean-
ness or sensuality to imbrute them."
H. D. Thoreau, "Higher Laws," Walden

Many of us have heard the story of the man who
served as the artist's model for a painting of Christ and
then, later in life, dissipated and fallen, became the
model for Judas. We have perhaps thought of people
we have known whose lives have shown the same
regression from their early potential to their sad deterioration.

Those who study the effects of aging make a statement something like this: The aged are what they were
when they were young—only more so. Only more so.
Smiling and cheerful—only more so. Sour and taci-
turn—only more so. Defeated and depressed—only
more so. Sometimes I have studied faces of young people
in my classes and wondered what they would look like
in old age. Their temperaments were sometimes easy to
predict, already hardened—what they were then, only
more so.

The thoughtful nature writer/philosopher Thoreau
spoke in almost Biblical tones of that temple-building
we all do on our own bodies, dedicated to the gods we
worship (God? alcohol? work? muscle tone? a special

talent?) in our own style. No other art we create can substitute for that. If our craft and materials are noble, beauty and nobility of spirit result. If our materials are corrupted by meanness, if our features reveal sensuality and a yielding to self-gratification, those qualities will imbrute them.

"What would happen if your face would freeze that way?" my mother would sometimes ask when my expression was grumpy. Let us find a mirror, shall we? And look into it carefully. What kind of expression has woven itself into our features? Will we be satisfied with the expression that will stay with us—only more so? Does it draw people to us or repel them—and will it—only more so? Will it help keep us from loneliness because its welcoming good cheer greets and attracts others? Or will the dour evasion and lack of expression keep others from us? This temple we build to the God we worship must be lit from within and provide an illumination for the setting that is ours as the years go by—only more so.

Lord, I long for your saving help to enable the windows of the temple I build in your honor to be illuminated by your love, not only as it is now, but more so. Amen.

Challenge: Make a point of looking in the mirror frequently the next few days, analyzing your common expression. Is it what you want to live with into the future—only more so?

A Noble Earthquake!

"So we will not be afraid, even if the earth is shaken / and mountains fall into the ocean depths;…" (verse 2).

"In Yosemite Valley, one morning about two o'clock, I was aroused by an earthquake; and though I had never enjoyed a storm of this sort, the strange, wild, thrilling motion and rumbling could not be mistaken, and I ran out of my cabin, near the Sentinel Rock, both glad and frightened, shouting, 'A noble earthquake!' feeling sure I was going to learn something."

John Muir, *"The Earthquake,"* <u>The Wilderness World of John Muir</u>

Because Psalm 46 is an "orphan psalm" (one with no recorded author), we cannot know who this brave person was who in behalf of God's people speaks such fearless words. I would likely have listened to him with awe: I frankly confess myself afraid of earthquake and ocean storm, albeit I have no personal experience with either. I am struck with awe at such evidence of vast tectonic plates of earth's crust sliding against each other, opening chasms and toppling mountains. And yes, I am afraid.

John Muir, the great naturalist of our western mountains, was a better match for the psalmist than I. Again and again in his writings he expresses his wonderment and awe at the natural phenomena he observed. In his startlement at the powerful convulsions of Yosemite's mountains, he is thrilled with "a noble earthquake" and a chance to learn something. Muir often seems, regardless of danger, confident that he is in a world that reveals the wonder of the One whose hand shaped it all. What he learns as he lives close to nature is the power and majesty of the Creator.

The psalmist's confidence, too, is in the presence and power of the supreme God. "God thunders, and the earth dissolves." One day the cone of Mt. St. Helens is there; the next it is not. In the face of that, how can I not be afraid?

Many factors determine how we react to fear. Some resist fear and refuse to give way to it. Others let it dominate their lives and determine their decisions. Some give way to utter panic. There is no use telling a person not to be afraid; a stronger individual with first-hand experience may be able to bring reassurance. Only when we can believe that the One who governs all things is our refuge can we relax in his mighty strength. Then we can know, as Moses assured the people of Israel, that "no god is like your God, riding in splendor across the sky, riding through the clouds to come to your aid. God has always been your defense; his eternal arms are your support" (Deut. 33:26-27). If physical dangers mean the end of my life here, those arms bear me safely into eternity. Like Muir, even from danger and storm, I can expect to learn something.

Lord of the earthquake, the volcano, and the lightning, I long for your saving help not to be afraid, because I know none of them can separate me from you. Amen.

Challenge: Examine yourself to discover the fear that bothers you the most. In your prayers, release that fear into God's hands and let him deal with it for you.

God's Generosity

"…he also made the stars" (verse 16).

"Look for the stars, you'll say that there are none;
Look up a second time, and, one by one,
You'll mark them twinkling out with silvery light,
And wonder how they could elude the sight."

William Wordsworth
"Calm Is The Fragrant Air"

Sometimes, especially in the fall, I look out over the lake in front of my house and, aside from a fishing boat in the distance, the surface looks completely unpopulated. But as I stand there enjoying the beauty, a loon calls, a duck bobs across a wavelet, and the white breast of a mewing gull catches the reflection of the sun. Suddenly the lake seems covered with bird life—and a fish jumps.

The evenings of my childhood on the edge of the North Dakota prairies were sometimes enhanced by the northern lights, fading and ribboning and changing color. Suddenly the sky was dark—until one noticed a strip of green near the horizon, or flares of red-orange high in the sky. Then it seemed as if there was color everywhere, never two minutes the same.

So, as Wordsworth had observed, with the stars. We have all known those evenings when seemingly no stars were visible until we had stayed in the darkness long enough, and then star after star after constellation gleamed before our surprised eyes and the sky was full of light.

Our observations of other people—and even ourselves—may have a similarity to the situations I have been describing. We see ourselves as bleak and drab and talentless, unless we look at ourselves through God's eyes as ones whom he loves and redeems. As the catchy saying insists, "God doesn't make junk." With surprise, we find talents and personality strengths we had never suspected. We are worth something after all.

And those others? The person whose gruffness and rudeness have led us to believe he has nothing to offer? We look at him more steadily and through the lens of the love God gives us to share. Soon we see a keen sense of humor, a rare generosity, or a talent we have never seen before.

He who "also made the stars," set the rainbow of the northern lights in motion, and populated the surface of the waters with the graceful birds and fish, has the same generosity in the talents and gifts he gives to us. We may look for these and say there are none, but as the poet suggests, if we "look up a second time"—and a third, and a fourth—we will wonder how these good talents and opportunities for service could elude our sight.

I long for your saving help, O Lord, to see the riches of opportunity and service you are able to make visible to me. Amen.

Challenge: When you seem able to see only limited graces of life in yourself and others, look around to see what you may be missing.

Ephesians 4:13-24

That Squalid Brood

"They have no part in the life that God gives, for they are completely ignorant and stubborn. They have lost all feeling of shame" (verses 18-19).

"Ignorance and her squalid brood. A universal dearth of intellect. Total abstinence from literature is very generally practiced....need I stop to remind you of the host of loathsome reptiles such a stagnant pool is fitted to breed! Croaking jealousy; bloated bigotry; carping suspicion; wormish blindness; crocodile malice."

William Gass
"In the Heart of the Heart of the Country"

Gass in his short story/essay gives us his view of the American small town (Indiana) through the eyes of a writer who has had a bad experience with romantic love and comes there to live. The child of poverty in the local school is belittled and falsely accused. Lonely Billy talks endlessly when he comes to the post office because it is the only time he gets a chance to use his voice. The real church of the community, the place where people really worship with enthusiasm, is the high school gymnasium at the Friday night basketball game. No one reads anything that is challenging or uplifting—in fact, they do not read at all.

Gass and St. Paul would, I suspect, have had fairly similar views on the effects of ignorance on a community or an individual. Both of them use strong language in portraying what ignorance does. Ignorance, Gass says, births a "squalid brood" of reptiles—"croaking jealousy, bloated bigotry, carping suspicion, wormish blindness, crocodile malice." Paul adds about such a brood that they "have lost all feeling of shame."

There is a kind of ignorance that God excuses because it comes from lack of opportunity to know better (Lev. 4), but the kind that Gass and Paul portray with such harshness is deliberate (note Paul's linking of ignorance and stubbornness). Ignorance has a brood of unsavory relatives that all too often keep it company.

We hear much about the importance of care and use of our bodies, of the nurture and development of our souls. There has often been a kind of divorce of mind and soul which has left the use and development of our minds out, as though body and soul are good but the mind is evil. The mind *is* often self-willed; it is not always willing to be yielded to God's control. But the human mind is also one of God's marvelous creations, complex and challenging beyond any man-made computer. God does not intend us to let it lie dormant, undeveloped, susceptible to the train of evils bred by ignorance and followed by shame. Most of us never begin to utilize the great potential of our brains. A vast spectrum of knowledge that stretches our thinking, enobles our behavior, delights our imagination, and corrects our ethics and our politics is as close to us as the wise choice of a book and the study of the Word in our Bibles. A mind petrified by disuse can be as evil a thing as a warped soul and a willfully-deformed body.

I long for your saving help, O Lord, to keep the evils that lurk in the path of ignorance far from me. Stimulate my mind as well as my soul and body for the sake of your eternal glory. Amen.

Challenge: Visit your church library to find a book that tells of someone who put his/her mind to work in the Kingdom. If you can't find one, ask your pastor to recommend one. (Suggestion: Charles Colson's *Life Sentence.*)

When God Goes Hunting

"You will walk with me, clothed in white" (verse 4).

> *"Alack, thou knowest not*
> *How little worthy of any love thou art!*
> *Whom wilt thou find to love ignoble thee*
> *Save Me, save only Me?*
> *All which I took from thee I did but take,*
> *Not for thy harms,*
> *But just that thou might'st seek it in my arms.*
> *All which thy child's mistake*
> *Fancies as lost, I have stored for thee at home;*
> *Rise, clasp My hand, and come!"*
> *Francis Thompson, "The Hound of Heaven"*

One of the most beautiful and moving poems in the English language is Francis Thompson's "The Hound of Heaven." Like a Swedish poem that uses a great fish pursuing its prey as a symbol of God, Thompson's poem uses the symbol of the hound, the hunting dog trained not to harm the prey but to hold it till the hunter can take over. The "I" of the Poem is likely the poet himself, knowing the love of "Him who followed, yet sore adread Lest, having Him, I must have naught beside." Yet, however he attempts to flee, "Fear wist [knew] not to evade as Love wist to pursue." Both the worlds of fantasy and of reality offer inadequate hiding places, he finds, for "Naught shelters thee, who will not shelter Me."

The fleeing soul seeks escape among children, but he is not fit company for them. He supposes he can find satisfaction in Nature, but she does not speak his language: "Heaven and I wept together, And its sweet tears were salt with mortal mine."

Eventually the Hound has done his work, and the soul is brought to bay, but not before youth is gone.

"I stand amid the dust o' the mounded years—
My mangled youth lies dead beneath the heap.
My days have crackled and gone up in smoke,
Have puffed and burst as sun-starts on a stream."

The fearful soul comes to understand that the Designer must "char the wood ere Thou canst limn with it," that it may even be there is little of life left before the trumpet from the "hid battlements of eternity" sounds the death note. Flight is no longer possible. He is stricken to his knees, waiting the stroke of judgment, defenseless, naked, tearful, trembling. If the present is so frightening, what can the future be?

Then all about him is the voice of the Hound of Heaven, speaking not in judgment but in love, not to condemn but to sympathize, to reassure. The only real hope of love is what He has come to offer. There is no one else to offer that kind of love. All that the soul has fancied as lost, has imagined he has left behind forever, is stored for him "at home," taken "not for thy harms, But just that thou mightst seek it in My arms." What the soul has looked upon as gloom is only the shadow of the great Hunter's caressing hand.

Great Heavenly Hunter, I long for your saving help that I may know the marvelous mercy behind your pursuit of me. Amen.

Challenge: Find a copy of the entire poem by Thompson, and read it aloud at least once a week for the next month.

Getting Bigger Inside

"But now I tell you: love your enemies and pray for those who persecute you,... " (verse 44).

"Keeping hatred inside makes you get mean and evil inside. We suppose to love everybody like God loves us. And when you forgive you feel sorry for the one what hurt you, you returns love for hate, and good for evil. And that stretches your heart and makes you bigger inside with a bigger heart so's you can love everybody when your heart is big enough. Your chest gets broad like this, and you can lick the world with a loving heart! Now when you hate you shrinks up inside and gets littler and you squeezes your heart tight and you stays so mad with people you feels sick all the time like you needs the doctor."

Margaret Walker, *Jubilee*

"Lick the world with a loving heart!" That's what Vyry does in Margaret Walker's beautiful novel *Jubilee*. Vyry is the black counterpart of Scarlett O'Hara in the period of the Civil War and the Reconstruction. Scarlett is the white daughter of a plantation owner. Vyry is also the daughter of a plantation owner—by his black slave. Scarlett is a woman of great physical beauty. Vyry is a woman of great spiritual beauty. Through all the deprivation and drudgery of her life, she maintains a dignity and nobility, even when the new house she and her husband have built after the war is burned down by the local Ku Klux Klan. When her family is almost beyond consolation and bitter feelings are almost impossible to overcome, Vyry's great spirit is able to feel pity for the poor twisted, misguided, hate-ridden men who have harmed them.

All of us have at some time known someone who has let his or her life or personality be soured and twisted by hatred or grudge. Whether he actually has been harmed by others or he only thinks he has, he lets the cancer of bitterness flourish. His personality—even his facial expression—changes and his disposition grows surly and sour.

Vyry, who is a keen observer and has seen what hatred has done to both blacks and whites, is too wise to let herself and her zest for life be infected with the disease of hatred, and she seeks to protect her family from its power. Using her vivid manner of expression, she talks of the One whose love brings about an expanded heart that, like hers, can include everyone. And she warns of the hate-filled mind that shrinks and squeezes the heart until spiritual heart trouble requires the calling of the medical doctor.

Being Christian does not mean we are free from hatred and the temptation to bitterness. It does mean we know the Doctor who can with his overwhelming love free us from hatred and the "heart trouble" it brings. Like Vyry, we know deep within us that "We suppose to love everybody like God loves us." We may find it hard to *like* everybody (does the Bible even ask us to do that?) but we know the Doctor who can turn our hatred into love. Then we can "lick the world with a loving heart."

I long for your saving help, O Lord, to deal with those deep negative feelings that seek to fasten their tentacles in my character. Set me free to love. Amen.

Challenge: Examine your own feelings honestly to discover any grudge or cherished hatred against anyone. If you find it, pray about it right now.

The Right Word

"What a joy it is to find just the right word for the occasion!" (verse 23).

But words are things, and a small drop of ink,
Falling like dew upon a thought, produces
That which makes thousands, perhaps millions, think.
Lord Byron, <u>Don Juan</u>

As Christians with a witness of love and salvation on our lips, we can appreciate what both the wise man and the poet have to say of the power of words when they are well chosen. Perhaps we are aware, too, of their weakness when they are poorly chosen, sputtering along replete with meaningless repetition, and of their danger when they are used to hurt and destroy.

One can hardly refrain from marveling that God could dare to put such a great message as his love and forgiveness into such a fallible vehicle as our human speech, into mouths that turn as easily to cursing and obscenity and mediocrity as they do to truth and reverence and nobility. So much language today is shoddy, imprecise, and full of the trivial—even among those who claim to be artists in its use. A columnist once suggested that his concept of hell was being condemned to listen to a replay of his conversations in this life in all their triviality. The ease with which even children and young people use language larded with profanity and gutter words is shocking evidence of the decadence around us.

We are sensible enough, usually, to show respect for a loaded gun. We don't keep arsenic in the refrigerator with the milk, or the disinfectant in the breadbox. We don't use a wood saw to cut metal or crystal. Yet these things are no more dangerous than words can be when wrongly or maliciously used. With the most important message in the world to spread to others, we need to develop real discernment and artistry in the use of words that make "thousands, perhaps millions, think." Then we will know "What a joy it is to find just the right word for the occasion" to tell those about us of the love God is extending to them. We do not need long Latinate words to tell God's goodness; we need simple clear words that themselves become vehicles of love.

> A word is a maverick being,
> Killing with a slow dull knife
> As easily as it gives hope
> In another context,
> The expression of the voice and face
> The handle that twists the knife.
>
> A word is a maverick being,
> Kindling with a bright delight
> As easily as it brings death
> In another context,
> The friendly intent of a kindly heart
> The match that lights the flame.
>
> R. Stenerson

We long for your saving help, O Father, that we may do your work in this world with our native language. We look forward to someday learning the language of heaven. Amen.

Challenge: Read the book of Proverbs noting the number of references to our words and speech.

Proud Words

"And the tongue is like a fire. It is a world of
wrong,..." (verse 6).

"Look out how you use proud words.
When you let proud words go, it is not easy to
*   call them back."*
                    Carl Sandburg, "Primer List"

Words are fascinating: they are powerful, they are useful, they are entertaining, intriguing. They can also be inadequate, trite, weak, and devastating. Some of those who use them are sensitive in their choice of words and can apply them like precision instruments; others pay little heed to them, fumble them, and throw them as aimlessly as a toddler throws a ball too large for him.

Both James and the poet Sandburg have observed how powerful words can be. Jesus is a master of words—his statements are deceptively simple, full of imagery and metaphor, compelling. They can be as soothing as "There are many rooms in my Father's house, and I am going to prepare a place for you" (Jn. 14:2), or as startling as "I came to set the world on fire, and how I wish it were already kindled" (Lk. 12:49).

Sandburg warns us against "proud words." The words we use give expression to the attitudes we have—one of which is pride. Even though we know we are warned against pride, we are even in our thoughts proud of our humility. The proud words follow—as we oh-so-subtly make sure our listeners appreciate our humility or recognize our accomplishments or admire our standing with others. Later we wonder why we talked so much, and know what the poet means when of proud words he says "it is not easy to call them back," those words by which we make sure our listeners see another person's pride or discount his abilities or deflate her joy in accomplishment.

James calls our speech a "world of wrong." He, too, is thinking of the "long boots, hard boots" with which our speech kindles the fires of resentment, anger, envy, hurt feelings. He has heard the strange blending of blessings and cursings that come from the same mouth. How often they come because of our desire to do as others do. Why should we imitate the most trite and unpleasant in the language of those about us? "Look out," not only how you use proud words, but how you use the ordinary ones, which when used with skill can enhance our witness, and when used as weapons can rival an artillery barrage.

I long for your saving help, O Lord, to use the gift of language rightly. Thank you for it and the way it makes communication possible. Help me to use it effectively and responsibly. Amen.

Challenge: Bad speech habits can make our communication ineffective. Examine yours to see if any detract from your Christian witness.

Cynic's Complaint

*"I have seen everything done in this world, and I tell
you, it is all useless. It is like chasing the wind" (verse
14).*

*"Our dried voices, when
We whisper together
Are quiet and meaningless...."*
                    T. S. Eliot, <u>The Hollow Men</u>

One of the most difficult puzzles of Scripture is the
book of Ecclesiastes. Its author is a spiritual brother of
Job at his points of impenetrable doubt and cynicism. It
is not strange that pious Hebrews sought to exclude the
book from the canon of their Scriptures. For every word
that is positive and faith-affirming, there are more that
are negative and make faith seem foolishness. "It is
useless, useless," said the Philosopher. "Life is all useless." T. S. Eliot, looking at the world of his day—and
ours—heard the same negation of substance and meaning in a world threatening to end "not with a bang but a
whimper." The whispers of his time and associates are
those of "hollow men." The author of Ecclesiastes knew
all about hollow men with voices that are meaningless.
Modern literature is replete with such voices.

Where does the believer fit into that picture of
futility, cynicism, and hollowness? We are people of
faith and confidence who believe life is good and God
controls all...aren't we? Our future is bright. What have
we to do with verses like "Enjoy every useless day of it
because that is all you will get for your trouble. Work
hard at whatever you do, because there will be no
action, no thought, no knowledge, no wisdom in the
world of the dead—and that is where you are going"

(Eccles. 9:9b-10). Who let that kind of thought into our Bible?

Strange though it may seem, it is in the face of such meaninglessness and cynicism that we raise our faith as our banner and cling to it, that we affirm that it is those who know they are hollow who can expect to be filled. We are told "All is uselessness" and we say in return that the judgment of what is use*ful* or use*less* is beyond what our minds can perceive. "After all this, there is only one thing to say: Have reverence for God, and obey his commands, because this is all that man was created for" (12:13). There is much about that I cannot understand, but I can grasp and hold on to it and be not hollow but fulfilled.

O Lord, who alone knows fully the meaning of my existence, I long for your saving help to make clear to me what I need to know about why you have placed me here. Amen.

Challenge: Read the book of Ecclesiastes, checking the statements you believe are stronger than the facts will support. Does that give you more reason for faith?

The Saintly Fool

*"To have faith is to be sure of the things we hope for,
to be certain of the things we cannot see" (verse 1).*

*"However, I resolved that I would always believe
what I was told. What's the good of **not** believing?
Today it's your wife you don't believe; tomorrow it's
God Himself you won't take stock in."*
                    Isaac B. Singer, "Gimpel The Fool"

None of us likes to be considered naive, gullible.
Isaac Singer's Gimpel is branded "the Fool" because he
is so easily taken in. From childhood on, he is told the
wildest tales and hooted at when he simple-mindedly
believes what he is told. When others tell him his parents have risen up from their graves, he goes off to see
for himself. The townspeople gull him; his wife gulls
him; never does there seem to be an end to his gullibil-
ity. We soon realize that he is one of the "holy inno-
cents" or "saintly fools" of literature.

For there is no meanness in Gimpel. He is hard-
working, quick to see the good in others—much as he
sees of their cruelty. He finds endless excuses why faith
is better than doubt. He is not stupid; he knows when
he is being made to look ridiculous. He has made a
conscious decision to be a man of faith in others, little as
they may deserve it. "I have resolved that I would
always believe what I was told," he explains. "What is
the good of not believing? Today it is your wife you
don't believe; tomorrow it is God Himself you won't
take stock in."

Simple Gimpel has stated a truth that far brighter
people than he have failed to realize. The hold of skep-
ticism grows quickly and spreads from a small spot to

cover an entire situation. Valid and sensible in one context, it touches one item of belief after another until we are suspicious of faith and fearful of being judged gullible and naive, resisting every statement of faith that comes to mind.

Only once in his life does Gimpel yield to the urge to seek revenge on those who ridicule him. He is too saintly a man to gain any satisfaction from it, and determines never again to yield to such temptation. We, too, will derive more satisfaction from a simple faith than from allowing our minds to be so faith-less and skepticism-filled that our predominant attitude becomes one of cynicism. Otherwise it may be for us, too, as Gimpel warns, that we begin by doubting the humans about us and end by not taking stock in God Himself. For it is by faith that we come to know Him.

I long for your saving help, O Lord, to make me a person of faith rather than a constant doubter. Amen.

Challenge: To whom in your life do you find it easy to respond with disbelief? Try to change your attitude toward that person to one of receptive faith.

A Good Name

"If you have to choose between a good reputation and great wealth, choose a good reputation" (verse 1).

"Good name in man and woman, dear my lord,
Is the immediate jewel of their souls.
Who steals my purse steals trash; 'tis something, nothing;
'Twas mine, 'tis his, and has been slave to thousands;
But he that filches from me my good name
Robs me of that which not enriches him,
And makes me poor indeed."

William Shakespeare, Othello

In Shakespeare's *Othello*, Cassio has been the object of a false accusation. Because of the accusation, Othello, who has recently made Cassio his first lieutenant, dismisses him from his employ. Cassio, in a conversation with Iago, his unknown accuser, who has slyly advised him not to take the matter seriously, grieves over his lost reputation. How can Iago fail to see the grievous harm some false accuser has done? What can replace his "good name"? What can be a greater loss than that good name? His possessions, in contrast, are temporary and trivial, mere "trash" compared to the confidence others have in him because of his good name.

Do we take a "good name" with equal seriousness in our day? Sometimes one wonders. Voters return to office candidates who have been convicted of dishonesty and deceit. Entertainers whose lives are an unholy mess are as popular and honored as those who have lived clean lives. Great honors are paid to those who have abused and made light of public confidence.

Yet for many of us, a clear title to a good name is important. Certainly, no one should be blamed for what someone else before him or near him has done to his name, but what we ourselves do by our characters to shape our reputation is highly significant. The seriousness with which our words are listened to—including those words by which we witness to our faith in Christ—depends on our good name. It is marvelous how the tarnished name of one who has gone wrong can with change and time be made clean again. It is also marvelous how in his mercy God gives us power to keep a good name for his glory.

In looking at the example of Jesus, we see one who again and again risked his good name to help those who along life's road had lost theirs. Our good name is not to be maintained by snobbishness or by holding ourselves above others, but rather by integrity and honesty. There may be an Iago in our lives who can damage our reputation, for a time at least, but like Job, Jesus, and Paul, we can still maintain our integrity, knowing that our good name is recorded safe from Iago in God's Book of Life.

My Lord, thank you that I may be called by your good name. I long for your saving help in treating that name with honor. Amen.

Challenge: Whom do you know that has been falsely accused and is in danger of losing his or her good name? What can you do to help?

Keeping the Faith

"How certain your promise is! How I love it!" (verse 140).

"There are still stars which move in ordered and beautiful rhythm. There are still people in this world who keep promises. Even little ones, like your cooking stew over your Bunsen burner. You may be in the middle of an experiment, but you still remember to feed your family. That's enough to keep my heart optimistic, no matter how pessimistic my mind, and you and I have good enough minds to know how very limited and finite they really are. The naked intellect is an extraordinarily inaccurate instrument."

Madeline L'Engle, <u>A Wind in the Door</u>

"Think-tank" is a new word in our day, though certainly the idea of intelligent people sitting down together to examine problems or plans for the future is not new. But one wonders if any brainstorming has ever resulted in such pessimism or gloom as is evident in our day. No matter what the subject being discussed— use of nuclear power, the economy, food supply, population growth, stress, loss of top soil—the conclusions seem to suggest doom and deprivation. Keen minds studiously applied to the problems make contradictory proposals and argue each other out of the possibilities for corrective action.

Doom is not the only answer to deep and provocative problems. In Madeline L'Engle's science fiction, her family of bright but ordinary youngsters and their scientist parents pit themselves against the invisible forces of evil that seek to depersonalize and destroy life on earth. Keenly intelligent as they are, this family knows that the "naked intellect is an extraordinarily inaccurate instrument." The nakedness of intellect needs to be clothed with the optimism of faith—faith in what we see and observe for ourselves. The universe is still a place of order and rhythm—natural law still operates. We are unusual indeed if we know no one whose promises can be relied upon, and if we can see no beauty in the world around us. If we have tested the promises of God we may not always be able to explain his acts but we can say "How certain his promise is!" Like Meg in L'Engle's story, we can let ourselves be used to thwart evil influences that X other people out, to affirm people over and over as individuals with worth of their own.

I cannot fulfill great promises to eradicate great universal problems on this earth. But I can be one of those who keep "cooking stew" over my Bunsen burner, keeping faith that many who are not only *as* faithful but *more* faithful promise keepers than I, are combining faith and intellect to overcome pessimism and doom. We are looking at "stars which move in ordered and beautiful rhythm," confident that in the face of the seemingly insurmountable hurdles humans face, the certain promises of God are still our dependable resources.

Lord, whatever the future holds, we are glad you have fast hold on our future. Amen.

Challenge: Examine your past to discover at least two instances when you were sure that disaster was ahead for you only to find that disaster was averted. Thank God again for those deliverances.

To Rise Again

"There is hope for a tree that has been cut down; it can come back to life and sprout" (verse 7).

"If the Father designs to touch with divine power the cold and pulseless heart of the buried acorn and to make it burst forth from its prison walls, will He leave neglected in the earth the soul of man made in the image of his Creator?"

W. J. Bryan, "The Prince of Peace"

As Job struggles with his grief over his loss of health, possessions, family, and peace of mind, and looks ahead to the death he expects, he turns to the same argument that humans have examined again and again: Since in nature resurrection follows seeming death year after year, will it not follow death in the life of human beings as well? Even an old stump when watered may sprout again as a sapling. "But a man dies, and that is the end of him; he dies, and where is he then?" (verse 10). In his pessimism he sees no hope in this life: "people die, never to rise. They will never wake up while the sky endures; they will never stir from their sleep" (verse 12). The ancient Hebrew Scriptures were slow to enunciate belief in a life after death.

To W. J. Bryan, the analogy between the "cold and pulseless" buried acorn in the frozen ground of winter and the spirit of man imprisoned in the dead human body is a valid one acceptable to faith. If the Father's design includes the enlivening touch of spring for the acorn, why is it not logical that it include the "spring" touch of resurrection for the soul of man made in the Father's image?

Theologians read various passages of Scripture with variant interpretations. Some speak of immortality, pointing to verses like John 10:28: "I give them eternal life, and they shall never die." Others emphasize resurrection, as Paul does in his letter to the Corinthian Christians (15:22): "For just as all people die because of their union with Adam, in the same way all will be raised to life because of their union with Jesus Christ." One cannot be raised from the dead if one has not been dead, they say.

Whether we take our place among those who avow faith in immortality or among those who believe that new life follows resurrection from the dead, we are among those who claim that the Father is the Lord of life and the victor over death and its cohorts. He has given us life and said, "No one can snatch them away from me."

"There is hope for a tree that has been cut down." There is also hope for life and resurrection in the experience of the human being. The Father will not "leave neglected in the earth the soul of man" made in his own image. That is our faith as Christians.

Lord of life, thank you that our faith includes eternal life with you. I long for your saving help to let that faith grow strong in me. Amen.

Challenge: Direct your Bible study this week to what the New Testament says about eternal life, death, and resurrection. What statement of faith results for you?

When Death Shall Die

*"There will be no more death, no more grief or crying
or pain. The old things have disappeared" (verse 4).*

*"Death, be not proud, though some have called thee
Mighty and dreadful, for thou art not so;…
Thou'rt slave to fate, chance, kings, and desperate
men,
And dost with poison, war, and sickness dwell,
And poppy, or charms can make us sleep as well
And better than thy stroke. Why swell'st thou then?
One short sleep past, we wake eternally
And Death shall be no more; Death, thou shalt die."*

     John Donne, "Death, Be Not Proud"

A coffin came to Sunday services one morning—
an empty one. Before it was brought to the chancel, the
congregational records of funerals conducted lying open
on its cover, the pastor who preceded it reminded us
that "He helps us in all our troubles so that we are able
to help others who have all kinds of troubles, using the
same help that we ourselves have received from God"
(II Cor. 1:4). This for us was an All-Saints remembrance.
The names of those added that year to the death-records
were read aloud. "Acknowledge, we humbly beseech
you, a sheep of your own fold, a lamb of your own
flock, a sinner of your own redeeming."[1]

 Surely that coffin was a reminder of death and the
inevitability of death visiting our congregational family
in the course of the church year, just as the fact that it
was an empty coffin reminded us of the Christian hope
of the resurrection. I hope no one found its presence

---

[1] *Lutheran Book of Worship,* p. 211

morbid. Facing reality is better than shunning it. It is better even for children to understand the reality of death within the family of God. But death one day shall die.

We walked past that coffin to kneel at the altar railing to take the bread and wine with which we receive the body and blood of our Lord, and again as we returned to our pews. One who was elderly put out his hand to steady himself by the coffin as he came down the chancel steps. Before many more years pass, another coffin at that spot will mark his home-going, and we will be reminded that "if we have been united with Christ in a death like his, we shall certainly be united with him in a resurrection like his."[2]

John Donne, a seventeenth-century English clergyman, expressed his confidence in the victory of resurrection over death in the above lines from a famous sonnet. Of course death is real, but its hold on the believer is temporary. Once that "sleep" is over, death shall be no more. It, too, shall die, never to trouble us again. It has no reason to be proud just as we have to be jubilant in our victory over it.

> I know of a sleep in Jesus' name,
> A rest from all toil and sorrow;
> Earth folds in her arms my weary frame
> And shelters it till the morrow;
> With God I am safe until that day
> When sorrow is gone forever.
>
> (LBW, 342)

I long for your saving help, O Lord, and praise you for replacing my fear with the hope of eternal victory. Amen.

Challenge: Read carefully the service for the burial of the dead in your congregational hymnal. Note the emphasis on hope and resurrection.

---

[2] *Lutheran Book of Worship,* p. 266

No Pat Answers

"Are you trying to frighten me?
I'm nothing but a leaf;
You are attacking a piece of dry straw" (verse 25).

But this [accident] invites the occult mind,
Cancels our physics with a sneer,...
                    Karl Shapiro, "Auto Wreck"

"It takes a lot of faith to maintain any serenity if you dwell on these sorrows," wrote a friend in her Christmas letter in the year when a friend had died after a three-year bout with cancer, a companion of her father's had been murdered, a colleague had been knifed to death, a friend lost a twenty-two-year-old son to cancer, and two valued older friends had died. How right she was! Each year adds some evidence to support her statement.

Shapiro in "Auto Wreck" describes the aftermath of an accident just after the ambulance pulls away with its sad load. The police take their notes, and the onlookers make trite comments about who was to blame. The persona of the poem thinks of the natural explanations of many deaths: deliberate in war, perhaps explainable in suicide and stillbirth. But why this "accident"? This brings forth the Job questions. "God, why would you attack a piece of dry straw like me?" And God never, never in the whole story explains to Job why his afflictions have come upon him. Job's plight, too, invites the "occult mind," cancels the rational explanations, and "splatters" our pat answers on bloody pavement.

But Job does not go unsatisfied. He is given his vision of Jahweh, vindicated and honored before his "comforters," even—in time—restored. The God who is infinitely above Job's human understanding is not the God of the instant pat answers, in spite of the many who claim to be his mouthpieces, offering glib solutions. But he is the God who does not forget his afflicted ones even when they rail against his justice. Job uses some strong language in his complaints against God. Many of the Old Testament saints did. But in the end, he was hushed before the vision of God that came by grace to answer his insistence on a hearing before God.

There are probably times when the pat answers apply accurately. Somehow, though, they are less than comforting, at the time at least. Particularly in those times when our physics goes askew and our explanations come off with a dull thud, we find the greatest comfort in remembering that God has not deserted us any more than he did Job.

Lord, I long for your saving help to enable me to cling close to you even when I don't know why I should. Amen.

Challenge: What question in your life do you find the most unanswerable? Tell God honestly that you are leaving the answer to him and simply holding on to him in faith.

The Unavoidable Web

"I have not come to do away with them, but to make their teachings come true" (verse 17).

"He learned that the world is like an enormous spider web and if you touch it, however lightly, at any point, the vibration ripples to the remotest perimeter and the drowsy spider feels the tingle and is drowsy no more but springs out to fling the gossamer coils about you who have touched the web and then inject the black, numbing poison under your hide. It does not matter whether or not you meant to brush the web of things. Your happy foot or your gay wing may have brushed it ever so lightly, but what happens always happens and there is the spider, bearded black and with his great faceted eyes glittering like mirrors in the sun, or like God's eye, and the fangs dripping."

Robert Penn Warren, <u>All the King's Men</u>

E. Stanley Jones, founder of the Ashram movement and author of many devotional books, speaks often of the moral law that is built into the very nature of the universe, moral law which humans can "break" only at their own risk. It is foolish to speak of humans breaking the law. Almost always the law breaks the human who ignores it. If I kill, I do not destroy the law against murder; I destroy my own well-being.

Most of us need to think more about the moral nature of the universe. God built into the nature of things the health created by love and the illness brought on by hatred. If I choose to nourish hatred in my heart, I do what can devastate my emotional and even my physical health. My nervous system is so planned and constructed that hatred takes its toll. Sin is not some trivial thing I can easily decide to ignore. People who work with individuals who cannot rid themselves from guilt know how deep the problems involved with it are—and know better than to say "Just forget about it."

Jack Burden, the narrator of *All the King's Men*, learns unforgettably the truth he expresses about the spider-web nature of human relationships and their inevitable consequences. He has assumed that he could blame these consequences onto the "great twitch" (the mechanistic interplay of psychology and fate) or the "great sleep" (escapist refusal to deal with what has happened), but he has to face the "great awakening" of accepting personal and individual responsibility for some shattering events. He has disturbed the web of the moral universe, and the spider of evil with its dripping fangs has struck.

The best that Jack can do is to correct what he can of the consequences of his acts and to live with a new moral awareness. That is all Penn Warren provides him power to do. How magnificent the mercy of God that receives the sinner in forgiving grace, that says "Neither do I condemn thee. Go and sin no more." Jesus came to fulfill the law on our behalf. He does not undo the consequences of all that we have done, but he can fulfill his promise of forgiveness and open to us newness of life—a life in accord with the moral universe in which his goodness has placed us.

Lord, I am so naive and unthinking about what your perfect goodness requires. I long for your saving help to live in a way that accords with what is best for me and what glorifies you. Amen.

Challenge: Take five minutes to examine your attitudes to make sure you are not cherishing what God's moral order cannot approve.

Real Freedom

"You will know the truth, and the truth will set you free" (verse 32).

"It fortifies my soul to know
That, though I perish, Truth is so;
That, howsoe'er I stray and range,
Whate'er I do, Thou dost not change.
I steadier step when I recall
That, if I slip, Thou dost not fall."

Arthur Clough,
"With Whom Is No Variableness"

Researchers who publish results of studies on stress or ability to deal with change, tragedy, and trouble frequently report that people with a deep commitment to faith and church fare better. It seems to me that condition may result from the confidence people of faith have that there are absolutes that can be depended on, to which we may link our lives. Granted, that is not a popular interpretation of reality today. Modern thought is more often relativistic and suspicious of absolutes. But as people of faith, while we may be skeptical of our ability to identify and define absolutes, we believe that God is; that good is ultimately what he defines it to be, and truth is as he established it.

Clough agrees. His words reveal the sense of freedom resulting from his conviction that "though I perish, Truth is so"; that God in essence does not change, though His actions in relation to us may change according to our responsiveness to Him. For example, in the Old Testament God "repented" when his people did. Clough believes that God stands firm even when human beings lose their balance. That truth has set him free.

Jesus promised his followers that the Helper, the Holy Spirit, the one "who reveals the truth about God" (Jn. 14:17), will help us to experience and live with that freedom. There are firm supports to which we can hold. All that imagery of God as rock, fortress, and refuge can be depended on, not because our feelings tell us so, but because the Spirit works in us the certainty of truth and freedom and eternity. How much of my life it took for me to accept that I was God's child not because my feelings said so but because God's Spirit speaking through the Word said so! Then the truth could set me free—over and over, no matter how bound up I became in doubt and uncertainty.

> Holy Spirit, truth divine
> Dawn upon this soul of mine;
> Word of God and inward light,
> Wake my spirit, clear my sight.
> Holy Spirit, peace divine,
> Still this restless heart of mine;
> Speak to calm this troubled sea,
> Stayed in your tranquility.
> Holy Spirit, right divine,
> King within my conscience reign;
> Be my guide, and I shall be
> Firmly bound, forever free.
>
> *(LBW, 257)*

Lord, thank you for the freedom that is grounded by your Spirit in your truth. I long for your saving help to live in that freedom today. Amen.

Challenge: The old saying is that everything changes but death and taxes. Write a better statement of your own that is based on God and his truth.

Two of a Kind

*"Look at me! I am eighty-five years old, and just as
strong today as I was when Moses sent me out"
(verses 10-11).*

*"I am a part of all that I have met;
Yet all experience is an arch wherethrough
Gleams that untraveled world whose margin fades
Forever and forever as I move.
How dull it is to pause, to make an end,
To rust unburnished, not to shine in use!
As though to breathe were life!"*

Tennyson, "Ulysses"

If characters from history and poetic narrative could
have a convention, what an interesting time Caleb and
Tennyson's Ulysses could have! They were two of a
kind. Caleb was one of the ten spies Moses sent to spy
out the land of Canaan to see if God's people could
successfully move in. It was a trip with high adventure.
Caleb, along with Joshua, returned with the positive
recommendation that the land was theirs for the taking.
("No," said eight other spies, to whom the people listened.) When the Israelites crossed into Canaan forty
years later, Caleb was one of the few of the original
generation left alive. When the conquered land was
divided among the families of Israel, whom do we find
requesting his portion in the hill country held by the
"race of giants called the Anakim...in large walled cities"? Caleb—then eighty-five years old!

Tennyson's "Ulysses" portrays another traveler—
a king whose journeys with high adventure lasted
twenty years and who, by the time he returned to his
wife, son, and island, was an old man. For a time all was

well, but before long, like Caleb, he wanted to be busy again. His son now ruled the kingdom. Ulysses was not needed. The old yearning for travel and adventure grew strong. There was more to be seen and experienced in that "untraveled world whose margin fades Forever and forever as I move." Ulysses found no joy in a life which failed "to shine in use."

I believe I am observing that those who retire most happily from their vocations are those who before that time comes have planned ahead for ways to "shine in use." We may not all feel as Caleb did about taking on a race of giants. But there is much to be done by those whose health makes activity possible. Volunteers in dozens of areas do important tasks to enrich the lives of others. *All* of us can learn *now* to be God's prayer warriors, that when days in which physical activities are fewer, we can know how to tap the power of prayer on behalf of others.

Lord, I know there is a sense in which "I am a part of all that I have met." I long for your saving help to make that part of me be a positive and helpful one, reaffirming life. Amen.

Challenge: Read about Abraham (Gen. 25), Moses (Deut. 31 and 34) and Joshua (Josh. 24) in their old age. Note how each accepts the end of life in terms of his faith.

"I Know of a Sleep"

"Our friend Lazarus has fallen asleep but I will go and wake him up" (verse 11).

"So live, that when thy summons comes to join
The immunerable caravan which moves
To that mysterious realm, where each shall take
His chamber in the silent halls of death,
Thou go not, like the quarry slave at night,
Scourged to his dungeon, but, sustained and soothed
By an unfaltering trust, approach thy grave,
Like one that wraps the drapery of his couch
About him, and lies down to pleasant dreams.

W. C. Bryant, *"Thanatopsis"*

We say we believe in a life after this one. We claim, even if we do not know its particulars, to believe it will be a life better than this one, free from grief or pain or death, forever in the presence of God who gave himself in love for us and has prepared a house of many rooms for us. Doesn't it seem a bit strange that, believing so, we find the death that releases us from this life and opens the door of resurrection life to us such an object of fear and sighing?

To a degree it is only natural because we associate death with thoughts of pain and separation. I am frankly suspicious when someone speaks of accepting the death of a loved one with grief transcended and a glow of joy. I'm sure that the shock simply hasn't hit yet. But just as often I wonder if our great mourning at the death of a believer isn't a kind of ignoring of our faith. Grief is natural; it can be healing. The reality of separation for a time needs to be faced and accepted. But we "sorrow not as those who have no hope." A Christian who has thought through his beliefs can pray "Make us certain that because he lives we shall live also, and that neither life nor death, nor things present nor things to come shall be able to separate us from your love which is in Christ Jesus our Lord, who lives and reigns with you and the Holy Spirit, one God, now and forever."[1]

Some may think it strange, but why should our service of homegoing not be a service of celebration for the gift of one we have loved and for all God has done for him or her? Is mournful music really as appropriate as "The Strife is O'er, the Battle Won"? How fitting the liturgical service in which all who have come participate by assuring each other "In sure and certain hope of the resurrection to eternal life through our Lord Jesus Christ, we commend to almighty God our brother/sister...."[2]

Jesus at Lazarus' dying and the poet Bryant both use the metaphor of sleep to describe one who "wraps the drapery of his couch about him, and lies down to pleasant dreams." And one day Christ will say about all his own, "I will go and wake him [her] up."

> I know of a morning bright and fair
> When tidings of joy shall wake us,
> When songs from on high shall fill the air
> And God to his glory take us,
> When Jesus shall bid us rise from sleep;
> How joyous that hour of waking! (LBW, *p. 342*)

I long for thy saving grace, O Lord, to develop in me a right attitude toward my own homegoing and those of the ones I love. Amen.

Challenge: Plan at least one part of your own homegoing service. Learn to think about it calmly and with joy in what your faith assures you of beyond this life.

---

[1] Romans 8:37-39, paraphrased

[2] *Lutheran Book of Worship*, p. 213

The Place of Prayer

"...and the door will be opened to him who knocks"
(verse 8).

You are here to kneel
Where prayer has been valid. And prayer is more
Than an order of words,..."
    T. S. Eliot, "Little Gidding," <u>Four Quartets</u>

Three decades ago I spent a summer in Europe, a summer in which one of my great joys was visiting some of the beautiful cathedrals of northern Europe. I can still feel the reverence which some of them inspired. Some left me unmoved because they seemed more like historical museums—worthy as those may be. But others made me long for nothing more than a quiet place in them where I could experience awe and reverence. When again I read the words of "Little Gidding," I said to myself "That was it. I was ready to 'kneel where prayer has been valid,'" where the atmosphere itself seemed hallowed by the presence of prayer—prayer that was "more than an order of words," a conscious act, or a vocal sound.

It was a blessing to be present where prayer has been valid for the generations who have come and gone through those ornate arched doors. "Prayer," I once heard the theologian Jaraslov Pelikan say, "has been the great corrective of the theology of the church." That result of prayer is bringing Christians together again in our day to be one in the Spirit.

It is also a blessing to be present in the parish church where prayer has been valid since its dedication until the present, offered by the congregation, by the groups that gather for study and petition, by those who welcome the infant in baptism, by those who say farewell to the aged in the service of homegoing, by those that bless the marriage, and by those who hold each other close in grief. The family of God shares all the experiences of life.

It is a blessing to be present in that meeting with the Father in our homes or offices where we listen and we speak, we praise and we weep, we bow in intercession and we search for guidance. In all of these places prayer has been valid not because of our skill in it but because God keeps his appointment with us in our need of and love for him. We may not be able to explain that validity in words that convince an unbeliever, but we have had our own experiences with that validity of prayer and have found that the One who gave us his promise has met us and been totally faithful.

> Lord, teach us how to pray aright,
> With reverence and with fear.
> Though dust and ashes in your sight,
> We may, we must draw near.
> We perish if we cease from prayer;
> O grant us power to pray,
> And when to meet you we prepare,
> Lord, meet us on our way.
>
> (*LBW*, 438, 1-2)

Challenge: Make a personal decision about a way to daily enrich your prayer life.

Dried Reeds and Cobwebs

"Godless men are like those reeds; their hope is gone, once God is forgotten" (verse 13).

"Tomorrow, and tomorrow, and tomorrow,
Creeps in this petty pace from day to day,
To the last syllable of recorded time;
And all our yesterdays have lighted fools
The way to dusty death. Out, out, brief candle!
Life's but a walking shadow, a poor player
That struts and frets his hour upon the stage
And then is heard no more: it is a tale
Told by an idiot, full of sound and fury,
Signifying nothing."

William Shakespeare, <u>Macbeth</u>

Bildad in the book of Job and Macbeth in the drama by his name make the same observation about the brevity of life. "Our life is short," says Bildad, "we know nothing at all; we pass like shadows across the earth." Macbeth, his ambition turned to bitterness, takes some of his images from Bildad. Life is a "brief candle," "a walking shadow, a poor player," "a tale told by an idiot, full of sound and fury."

Much that Bildad says to the sufferer is no help to Job. He reiterates the old notion that the cause for suffering can be easily identified in the sin of Job or his children. Bildad is one of those "comforters" bidden by God at the end of the story to ask Job to pray for him for "You did not speak the truth about me as Job did" (Job 42:8). Yet his image of the person who tries to support himself by leaning on a dried up reed or a spider web is valid. Such supports cannot make him stand erect. His "hope is gone, once God is forgotten."

Macbeth at the beginning of Shakespeare's play is a noble man, respected and honorable. But at its end he is a toppled ruin—a murderer whose first murder has led him to kill again and again, one who is friendless, dehumanized, whose only comment when he hears of his wife's suicide is that she should have found a more convenient time. Macbeth has tried to lean his weight upon dried reeds and cobwebs, and life has become only "sound and fury, signifying nothing."

Our great temptations and trials are likely less traumatic than those of either Job or Macbeth. But in our lives, too, come the times when we have to choose what we will lean upon—the God to whom Job even in his worst moments held fast ("Though he slay me, yet will I trust in him" [13:15, RSV]), or the dried reeds and spider threads of Macbeth. If it is true that "Hope is gone, once God is forgotten," then it is also true that "hope is restored, once God is remembered." In that lies our hope.

Lord God, thank you that life for me can be more than "a tale told by an idiot, full of sound and fury." I long for your saving help to fill it with your purpose and meaning. Amen.

Challenge: Read all the speeches of Bildad in the book of Job (8, 18, 25, 26:5-14). Why does God in 42:8 reject Bildad's interpretation of divine justice?

Excuses, Excuses

"I know that good does not live in me—that is, in my human nature. For even if the desire to do good is in me, I am not able to do it" (verse 18).

"Ay, there were soberer accidents that might destroy him: if, for instance, the house should fall and imprison him beside his victim;…These things he feared: and in a sense, these things might be called the hands of God reached forth against sin. But about God himself he was at ease; his act was doubtless exceptional, but so were his excuses, which God knew; it was there and not among men, that he felt sure of justice."

       R. L. Stevenson, "Markheim"

In R. L. Stevenson's short story, "Markheim," the man who has just murdered the pawnbroker seeks the money he intends to steal, rationalizing as he does so that so long as no unexpected "accidents" take his life or reveal him to the forces of justice, all will be well. God he need not fear: "about God himself he was at ease; his act was no doubt exceptional, but so were his excuses, which God knew;…" When a messenger of God, disguised as a tempter, faces him, one of the hardest tasks the messenger must accomplish is to persuade Markheim that his excuses will not hold before God. Day by day, Markheim's life has grown more evil, his excuses less valid. Forced to face himself honestly for once, Markheim gives himself up to the police.

As humans, most of us are skillful at coming up with reasons for our actions which we are confident will impress God. Surely he could not be so rigid as to fail to see our logic. Why, anyone would have lost her temper, given the provocation I had! Of course God will not only understand. He will share my indignation! As far as my criticism of the soloist on Sunday, isn't it understandable that we want what is done in the church to be really top quality? That music surely couldn't have sounded very good to One used to the music of heaven! As for snarling at the children when they interrupted the television football game, who wouldn't have done that?

As for taking a look at my life-style to see if I couldn't give more to relieve world hunger, I'm sure God understands that in my profession I have to have a nice home and good clothes and—well, he knows that I am already giving to the congregation and to the community causes in which others expect me to contribute. And I'm sure he knows I'm too tired by evening to visit those people that just moved into the next block. "It is there, and not among men, that I feel sure of justice."

One of the surprises of heaven will be our new vision of the holiness and justice of God. What a miracle it will seem to us then that we have come to know him even more as a God of love and mercy!

I long for your saving love, O Lord, to make me honest. Help me to see through my own rationalizations to know how inadequate they are. Amen.

Challenge: Set aside a few quiet moments to explore your own rationalizations, to find one that has become a habitual response of yours—and dispense with it.

Walking Openly

"If your brother sins against you, go to him and show him his fault. But do it privately, just between yourselves" (verse 15).

"Only the brave know how to forgive....A coward never forgives; it is not in his nature."
Lawrence Sterne, <u>Sermons</u>

There is something about showing another person his fault against us privately that doesn't fit the way we ordinarily do things. We seem to receive more satisfaction from showing other people someone's fault and doing it publicly. Perhaps Laurence Sterne, an author/ clergyman of two centuries ago, is right in suggesting that it takes courage to deal directly with someone who has wronged us. That face-to-face encounter has much to do with our ability to really forgive, and "Only the brave know how to forgive. A coward never forgives;..."

The ability to be truly honest with others is hard to develop. It seems to involve all our insecurities. We fear having our words challenged as dishonest or distorted, or having them encounter an accusing silence, especially if the issue is reduced to one person's word against another's. We fear the other may react with hostility, leaving us standing alone and isolated. We fear observers may find us blunt, troublemakers in a circle of friends. We fear countercharges which may make us appear guilty. It is hard for us to be that open with others.

Openness with others does not come easily. Even among members of our families and close friends, openness takes courage and a willingness to be vulnerable. If we try to be open with others who have erected a wall between them and us, we feel exposed. Yet we know from experience that few things are more uncomfortable than someone else's newly erected wall between him and us, especially if we do not understand the reason for it. Words like super-sensitive, touchy, or paranoid seem to surround our relationship with the person.

How far more healthy the results where honesty and openness can govern the relationship! Matthew, an ex-tax collector, had likely experienced many angry accusations, as had the impulsive Peter. Jesus knew these men who would walk in his kingdom would need to learn to walk openly, courageously. Paul rebuked Peter for his shunning of gentile Christians. He did it openly—which must have taken courage (the ex-persecutor rebuking the big fisherman, known for his impetuous speech). Like them, we are to be open in our dealings with each other.

I long for your saving help, O Lord, to make me to be open, courageous, and loving in my relationships with your other children. Amen.

Challenge: Is there someone with whom your relationship is awry because of "locked jaws"? Make the occasion to speak to him or her and really forgive.

The Habit of Praise

"I will proclaim your greatness, my God and king; I will thank you forever and ever" (verse 1).

"The world is charged with the grandeur of God.
It will flame out, like shining from shook foil;..."
Gerard Manley Hopkins, "God's Grandeur"

"Charged," as it is used in Hopkins' poem extolling "God's Grandeur," is a word from the field of power and electricity, referring to a storing or accumulation of force and energy. The whole world, he suggests, is vibrant with the living energy and force of God's power and awesomeness. At times the grandeur flashes out so that we are especially aware of it, as we are of the sun's striking a sheet of aluminum foil. At other times the sense of it accumulates gradually until it overpowers us.

Is one of the reasons the psalms are among our favorite devotional reading that they, too, are charged with the writer's sense of God's grandeur and praiseworthiness? The last six psalms rise in a crescendo of praise. Individual, city, nation, and universe are called upon to sing the praise of God, to express it in dance and with musical instruments, until all of sound is one great hallelujah to God in his temple.

Are we practiced in praise? Which comes more easily for us—praise or complaint? Every morning and every nightfall is an occasion to bring God praise that has grown out of the day's experience. Never until I experienced continual shortness of breath did I give nightly praise for the deep easy breathing medication made possible. Not till I experienced friends who would give me room to be myself without rejecting me for my imperfections did I come to praise God regularly for his acceptance of me "just as I am." In praise we find the joy and exuberance of healthy spiritual growth. In forgetfulness of praise we lose our spiritual zest and energy.

There is no denying that at times we face tasks and trials that threaten to make praise seem impossible. How can we sing praise in the face of illness or the death of one we love? Can we see the grandeur of God in a world full of poverty and the madness that threatens war? Can we feel our independence fading in the face of old age and still praise the Lord? In all of these we can give praise to God for his presence, for his compassion, for his preparing a future for us. Through such praise we sense the strength and joy his Spirit gives us as it touches our spirit and assures us of his everlasting arms around us.

I long for your help, O Lord, to develop the spirit of praise and a sense of the grandeur of the world you have given us to enjoy. Amen.

Challenge: Work at developing a habit of beginning and ending each day with an expression of praise for the wonder of God's presence and gifts in your life.

Clean Spittoon

*"If anyone makes himself clean from all those evil
things, he will be used for special purposes, because he
is dedicated and useful to his master, ready to be used
for every good deed" (verse 21).*

> *"Hey, boy!*
> *A clean spittoon on the altar of the Lord....*
> *At least I can offer that."*
>> *Langston Hughes, "Brass Spittoons"*

How does one glorify God if one's job is to wash a
filthy spittoon? or to empty bedpans? or to pick up the
garbage? to mop up the mess after someone else? Black
poet Langston Hughes speaks to and for those whom
society often keeps in despised, menial tasks. Perhaps
more of us think of the menial parts of our own jobs,
which often seem tiresome or repulsive to us. "A clean
spittoon....At least I can offer that."

How often we fail to be aware of the many people
who keep our world livable by the unseen, unsung,
unpleasant tasks they do quietly, uncomplainingly! How
many homes smell good, wear well, and are in repair—
both physically and spiritually—because their inhabit-
ants are willing to do what no one else notices!

Writers who have attempted to envision Paul's
origins usually imagine his coming from a well-to-do
home. Whatever is true in that respect, the unmarried
Paul had looked about at the pottery and dishes and
noted their variety, each made for a purpose, whether
for special or ordinary occasions. Hughes has no doubt
seen those who wash dishes, polish shoes, act as door-
men, and clean the public areas of business places. How
does one honor God in that kind of situation?

A river-boat worker explained the spotlessness of his engine-room by saying "I've got a glory." "A bright spittoon on the altar of the Lord" might sound like a grotesque combination, but if that bright polishing was the worker's task, he was right to assume that in it God could be glorified. It is not so much *what* we do for God as the love and the care with which we do it that counts. The restroom in the church of God should be as clean as the chancel.

There is something in the work each of us does that is less pleasant than the rest. Cleaning the oven is less satisfying than stirring up the birthday cake. Correcting a monotonous set of papers is less interesting than presenting an ego-satisfying lecture in class. Collecting delinquent bills is no doubt harder than counting up brisk sales. Cleaning the barn is drudgery compared to displaying a prize sow. Kissing a sweet clean baby is something else than cleaning up after an incontinent patient. But "A clean spittoon on the altar of the Lord....At least I can offer that."

O Lord, *remind me that the most tiresome drudgery can be placed in your hands as my offering. Amen.*

Challenge: Take on yourself for a week an unpleasant task which will cheer the spirits of someone near you whose work is menial and dull.

The Victory Achieved

"It is better to be patient than powerful. It is better to win control over yourself than over whole cities" *(verse 32).*

"Reckon the days in which you have not been angry. I used to be angry every day; now every other day; then every third and fourth day; and if you miss it so long as thirty days, offer a sacrifice of thanksgiving to God."

Epictetus
"How the Semblance of Things are to be Combated"

I remember as a young person reading Benjamin Franklin's *Autobiography* and being greatly impressed with the determined and businesslike method by which he attacked what he saw as his faults. One by one he set out to eradicate them, to weed them out of his personality and character, daily keeping track of his successes and failures. It served to stimulate my feelings of inadequacy far more than to inspire me to success. If young Benjamin could succeed so valiantly in doing what he thought was right and admirable, why was I such a dud at being patient, at controlling my temper, at being loving? I felt far more as if verse 22 ("Trying to educate stupid people is a waste of time") rather than verse 32 were directed at me. I wasn't sure either Franklin or I were going to find success in that area of life.

The words of Epictetus seemed an echo of Franklin. Get out the score card again, and keep track of the days. Not much danger, I thought, of my getting to the thirtieth angerless day at which I should begin a "sacrifice of thanksgiving." I'd be happy with a week, let alone an entire month. Why, I'd even have to give up typing to get that far!

But is this really the method God intends me to use? Does he want his children busy recorders of their successes or failures, or does he want their eyes confidently fastened on him, praising him for every victory and waiting for the sanctifying power of his Spirit to make those victories more frequent?

Humility can be a false variety of virtue. We keep bemoaning our same faults, never taking time to evaluate what God is doing within us. If we have asked him to give us victory, shouldn't we expect that overcoming power to be granted? It is not pride to observe that I am more patient now, that I lose my temper less often. Sanctification is his work within us, not the conscientious marking of a score card. It involves faith that when we pray that the fruit of the Spirit may grow in our lives, those seedlings will appear and grow and bear a harvest—a harvest that will be visible even to us as the days go by. My apologies, good Benjamin, but I don't find your score card good Christianity.

Lord, I long for your help to create holiness in my life. May I see its fruit in my disposition, the result of your grace in me. Amen.

Challenge: Ponder what fault you yearn most avidly to have erased from your daily life. Turn it continually over to him—and watch joyfully for the results.

How Short Our Life Is!

*"A thousand years to you are like one day; they are
like yesterday, already gone, like a short hour in the
night" (verse 4).*

*"Time has no divisions to mark its passage, there
is never a thunder-storm or blare of trumpets to
announce the beginning of a new month or year. Even
when a new century begins it is only we mortals who
ring bells and fire off pistols."*
Thomas Mann, <u>The Magic Mountain</u>

"Teach us how short our life is, so that we may
become wise." (verse 12).

Do we deliberately push away from us those experiences that remind us of the brevity of life?—the time
when we intended to read just a little more of a good
book but found the clock past midnight before we realized how hours had slipped past; the "just a few minutes" of good conversation at the end of a visit that
turned into an hour; the day when we intended to visit
sick friends but were swamped in our petty errands
until the day was done. Lord, "teach us how short our
life is"—"like a short hour in the night."

Why is it so important that we remember life's
brevity? Isn't it that we may assess our values and set
our priorities in a way that is wise? How often do we
make our decisions of "Yes, I will" or "No, I'd rather
not" on the basis of what will be important beyond
death? How often in terms of what is comfortable right
now? Which of my investments will bear interest once
the casket is paid for?

Why remember life's brevity? Isn't it also that we
may set our pace sensibly in the light of what we have

to do? It is comforting to know that God is not finished with me yet, but I come to see how much of my time has been spent doing what has profited neither others nor myself, let alone Him. That does not mean that we are not to take time for relaxation, pleasure, or refreshment: those, too, are in his plan. But it does remind me that my time is one of my gifts to God (who gave it to me first), and that his priorities in its use should be mine. If those of us in the church ever really acted on that premise, we'd send our pastors scrambling to find work enough for us to do.

One of the signs of passing years in my life has been an increasing sense that time is speeding up. The bookmark in my devotional book moves relentlessly forward. The six-year-old I haven't seen for a couple of years turns out to be one of this year's high school graduates. But if the time I have left is used to fulfill priorities of which God approves, I can make of that time a fruitful experience and a time of zestful living.

"Fill us each morning with your constant love,
so that we may sing and be glad all our life"
(verse 14).

Singing goes with serving and a sense that I am using my time according to God's priorities.

Lord, we know it is true that "life is soon over, and we are gone." I long for your saving help that I may leave behind me rich years of service produced by my keeping time with what you think is important. Amen.

Challenge: Make a careful study of the next two days to observe how you are using your time. When you have the results before you, do you feel good about your use of time?

Plagued

"I am in trouble, God—listen to my prayer! I am afraid of my enemies—save my life!" (verse 1).

"And indeed, as he listened to the cries of joy rising from the town, Rieux remembered that such joy is always imperiled. He knew what those jubilant crowds did not know but could have learned from books: that the plague bacillus never dies or disappears for good; that it can lie dormant for years and years in furniture and linen-chests; that it bides its time in bedrooms, cellars, trunks, and bookshelves; and that perhaps the day would come when, for the bane and the enlightenment of men, it would rouse up its rats again and send them forth to die in a happy city."
Albert Camus, <u>The Plague</u>

In his novel *The Plague,* Albert Camus portrays a siege of bubonic plague in Oran, a North African city, from the time when the dying rats appear everywhere, to the final cessation of the deaths and the rediscovery of the joy of living. Each citizen must find his (the characters are almost only men) way of relating to the plague, obviously an analogy to evil in human experience. Dr. Rieux, with professional dedication, tries to alert the authorities and uses his medical skills in a usually futile ministry to the infected and dying. Tarrou, the journalist, thinks it enough to write an account of the plague until finally he is driven to join Rieux in his work—and dies. The authorities try to deny the presence and the seriousness of the plague until they have no choice but to arrange for the death carts and the burials. Some hide in terrible isolation; others seek comfort in drunken socializing. Grand, the would-be-novelist, gives up his attempt to make the first sentence of his masterpiece perfect in order to keep the grim statistics of the casualties. Father Paneloux, in the face of watching a child die, gives up his judgmental preaching that the plague is the result of the wickedness of the people. Cotard tries to grow rich exploiting the situation. Rambert wants to flee, but at the last moment, is compelled to stay and aid Rieux.

Finally the plague subsides, and in great relief the people again know the goodness of life. But always, as the quote above indicates, there is the awareness that the plague has not disappeared for good. Somewhere it hides, waiting the right conditions to emerge again and wreak its havoc, in another time and perhaps another place.

How like the existential human experience with evil! We, too, react as Camus' characters do—trying to ignore it; keeping statistics of it in others; judging the responsibility for it; succumbing to its ravages; seeking to grow rich from it; seeking to flee its presence; doing what we can to fight it.

One thing the psalmist knows to do that Camus' characters do not. He can pray in faith to a God who is concerned about his people. "All righteous people will rejoice because of what the Lord has done. They will find safety in him; all good people will praise him."

The survivors in Oran do learn something, though, from their terrible experiences, something worth knowing: "There are pestilences and there are victims, and it's up to us, as far as possible, not to join forces with the pestilences" (p. 229).

Lord, I long for your saving help that I may not join forces with the pestilences in this world but, knowing that my only safety is in you, do what I can to help the victims. Amen.

Challenge: Analyze the way in which the people in your community relate to the presence of evil. Are their methods comparable to those of the people of Oran? How do you yourself respond?

Romans 6:15-23

Split Personality

"What did you gain from doing the things that you are now ashamed of? The result of those things is death" (verse 21).

"Within my earthly temple there's a crowd.
There's one of us that's humble; one that's proud.
There's one that's broken-hearted for his sins,
And one who, unrepentant, sits and grins.
There's one who loves his neighbor as himself,
And one who cares for naught but fame and self.
From much corroding care would I be free
If once I could determine which is Me."
Edward S. Martin, "Mixed"

In Fyodor Dostoevsky's portrayal of a fragmenting personality, *The Double,* the afflicted character Golyadkin becomes convinced that a man identical to himself is supplanting him at his job and in his social relationships. As his condition grows worse and finally leads to his commitment to an institution, he finds himself surrounded by a plague of little Golyadkins pursuing him and leaving him totally bereft of the uniqueness of his identity. In Martin's poem above, the persona has a version of the same problem. The humble, contrite, loving character must face the proud, unrepentant, self-centered aspect of his or her own personality, and know that side is as validly present as the other.

Martin's poem is not great poetry; it lacks subtlety. But the truth it expresses can hardly be questioned. The one who has not yet experienced the "moment of truth" in which he must admit "I don't do the good I want to do; instead, I do the evil I don't want to do" (Rom. 7:19) has a long way yet to go. Our moral confusion often has to do with sorting out who among Martin's characters we are.

Fortunately our text does not end where Martin's poem ends. It goes on to reassure us that although the moment of truth has shown us our slavery to that which we deplore, we can be set free. Oddly, we can be set free, Paul says, from slavery to sin to accept willingly and gladly another kind of slavery—to righteousness. Outside of Christianity, that makes no sense at all. But our behavior within that new kind of slavery will never embarrass us, never surround us with "corroding care." Sin, on the other hand, pays its wages—death.

Now we face a new life. "But now you have been set free from sin and are the slaves of God. Your gain is a life fully dedicated to him, and the result is eternal life....God's free gift is eternal life in union with Christ Jesus our Lord."

Now I can determine "which is me." "My earthly temple" is no longer crowded. That space belongs to Master and servant. If it is invaded by those who "unrepentant, sit and grin," I can with Christ's authority say "Be gone!"

O Lord, I long for your saving help that I may no longer do those things that result in shame and death. May I instead live as your love-servant. Amen.

Challenge: Look frankly at your life today. Identify one event in it that has threatened to give an intruding sin room and tell it firmly "Out! Out! I am no longer your servant."

The Setting Isn't Exclusive

"I look to the mountains;..." (verse 1).

"But for my children, I would have them keep their
distance from the thickening center; corruption
Never has been compulsory,..."
     Robinson Jeffers, *"Shine, Perishing Republic"*

Riding in a tour bus through the Grand Teton Mountains, I listened to our guide tell us that those mountains had been purchased by John D. Rockefeller and presented to the United States to be preserved as a national park. My response was an almost hilarious burst of laughter at the idea that those great humps of rock with their majestic crests could be owned by any human being, no matter how wealthy. (I also appreciated that one so wealthy wanted to preserve them for his fellow citizens.)

There is something about mountains—something that moves and stills us, that challenges us to think reverently and with a catch in our breathing. To the psalmist, they seemed a source of security and assurance of help. To Jeffers, yearning for a refuge for his children from corruption, from the "thickening center" in which crime and sleaziness and inhumanity are rampant, the mountains represented a place of escape and cleanness.

Some would look upon Jeffers' association of the cities with corruption and the mountains with health and cleanness as romantic twaddle. But perhaps the most important thing he says in "Shine, Perishing Republic," is that "Corruption never has been compulsory...." We have a great tolerance today for corruption, a tendency to excuse it and pretend its danger can be reduced by simply ignoring it. Karl Menninger addresses this issue in his book, *Whatever Happened to Sin?* He warns against our assumption that evil can be handled by ignoring it, by supposing that its consequences can be eroded by belittling them, pretending they don't exist.

It is true that "corruption never has been compulsory." If we care for the human race and even for ourselves, someone must deal with the monster rather than run from it. It is not enough to head for the mountains, gleaming though their peaks may be. Corruption is possible—and probable—anywhere humans reside. It needs to be identified and eradicated both in the turmoil and the trash of the city and along the trails of humans in the mountains. Government officials in our day spend much time and concern on what to do with toxic waste so generations to come are not poisoned by its residue. As Christians, we should be even more concerned that our toxic moral wastes do not make ours a world in which spiritual health is stunted and poisoned.

Lord of the city slum and the mountain wilderness, make us more willing to be involved in the struggle against this world's toxic spiritual wastes. Amen.

Challenge: Do your best to identify the most destructive form of corruption in your community and become one of those who oppose rather than tolerate it.

Flirting with God

"Before you sold the property, it belonged to you; and after you sold it, the money was yours" (verse 4).

"He made [money]" said Mr. Dooley, "because he honestly loved it with an innocent affliction. He was thrue to it. Th' reason ye have no money is because ye don't love it for itself alone. Money won't iver surrinder to such a flirt."

Peter Finley Dunne
Mr. Dooley On Making a Will

Peter Finley Dunne uses his humorous character of Mr. Dooley, a talkative Irish-American, to make shrewd and perceptive comments on life in an earlier part of our century. As did Dunne himself, Dooley saw a nation of rapid growth (today's corner house is tomorrow's supermarket), with its people—at least most of them—in headlong pursuit of the American dream, whatever that was. Much of it was the love of money, which Dooley says was loved with an "innocent affliction" [affection]. The character he speaks of in this quotation did make money because he was "thrue [true] to it." Dooley's listener, on the other hand, has little money "because ye don't love it for itself alone." Money will not "surrinder to such a flirt."

Ananias and Sapphira in our text from Acts were "true" to their love of money in those days when the early believers were experimenting with communal living. Evidently torn between that love of money and their desire to be part of the Christian community, they sold some property and gave part of the return to the communal treasury. Perhaps finding it hard to have faith that they would never need a nest-egg, they withheld a part of the sales price. In doing so, they violated no law. As Peter tells them, the property had been theirs; the sales price was theirs. No one had the right to take it from them. Why, then, does the story have such a terrible ending? Because they lied about what they had done, claiming to have given the full amount. Of their money it can be said, "they loved it with an innocent affliction" that led them to guilty lying.

Money is one matter when we look at it in terms of what it can provide for our needs and what it can do for others who are needy. It is another matter when it makes Silas Marners of us, gleefully counting up money for its own sake, yet pretending to be too modest in our income to be able to share with others. "You cannot serve God and mammon," Jesus warns his followers. "For your heart will always be where your riches are" (Lk. 12:34). Money, says Dooley, "won't iver surrinder to such a flirt." God, too, calls for full allegiance. Neither will he be satisfied with our flirting with him.

Lord, help me never to be a flirt in my commitment to you. I long for your saving help that I may willingly surrender all you have given me back into your hands. Amen.

Challenge: Re-study your financial commitment to the Kingdom of God. Does your giving at present call for upward adjustment?

To Be Taken Seriously

"Whoever welcomes in my name one such child as this, welcomes me" (verse 5).

"The greatest reverence is due a child!
If you are contemplating a wicked act,
despise not your child's tender years."
Juvenal, <u>Satire XIV</u>

Any person or family or church or society which fails to give regard to its children is short-sighted. The future of any of these units can be no brighter than its children. What an awesome responsibility has been laid on those who bring them into the world! Yet some people seem to bring these little ones into the world where they must struggle and often suffer, with no more thought than if they were bringing home a pet from a pet shop. And even in what we would like to call our advanced age, child abuse is not only practiced, but is a major problem.

Juvenal, a writer of ancient Rome, says much the same as Jesus in his warning to adults about the treatment of children: "The greatest reverence is due a child." Jesus goes beyond that, to "assure you that unless *you change* and become like children, you will never enter the Kingdom of heaven." Even more, the *great* in the Kingdom must be like children. To welcome the child is to welcome Christ himself.

What is it about children that makes them great? Jesus points to this when he speaks of their faith (verses 6-7). Their faith—their simple, accepting and trusting faith. The "greatest reverence due a child" is respect for its faith. How terrible for the world that there are things that make people (not only children) lose their faith.

The parent who takes life lightly or is abusive destroys the child's faith in one who should be his greatest help in life. Jesus says, "How terrible for the one who causes" a loss of faith in God in a child or young person. Faith can be a fragile thing, shattered by flip talk or taunts about those people a young person respects. I have always believed that James' reason for saying "My brothers, not many of you should become teachers" (3:1) was his realization of how easily the desire of a teacher to appear learned causes him or her to belittle a simple faith—even unintentionally. Conversely, what reinforcement a teacher who is a person of faith can be to faith in others!

"See that you don't despise any of these little ones." The great teachers of all ages and many cultures are clear about that. So should we be. We need to seek for ourselves the simple faith they illustrate if we would be part of the Kingdom.

> Your little ones, dear Lord, are we,
>   And come your lowly bed to see;
> Enlighten every soul and mind,
>   That we the way to you may find. Amen.
>
> (*LBW*, 52)

Challenge: Look for a way in which you personally can find a way to reinforce the faith of a young person in your circle of friends.

The House of Prayer

"I assure you, they have already been paid in full"
(verse 5).

"Wherever God erects a house of prayer,
The Devil always builds a chapel there;
And 'twill be found, upon examination,
The latter has the largest congregation."
　　　　Daniel Defoe, "The True-Born Englishman"

Whether God's house of prayer or the devil's chapel gets the largest congregation I have no way of knowing, unless I accept Daniel Defoe's word for it. But I do know that I need to use caution to keep out of the chapel. Surely it is to the advantage of the evil one to open the chapel door and usher me in. In fact, he is not above beckoning me right out of the house of prayer to urge me into his chapel.

Someone has written, "Satan trembles when he sees/The weakest saint upon his knees." He not only trembles. He acts to be sure that such kneeling is in his chapel rather than in God's house of prayer. One of his techniques is to make us eager to be seen in prayer by others. The house of prayer is usually a private place, though God's people are often enriched by praying together. In contrast, Satan's chapel has ample window space so that everyone may see his devotees.

Another popular device for prayer in Satan's chapel is the use of "a lot of meaningless words." It fits our human belief that "quantity must surely ensure quality" to "think that God will hear because their prayers are long." Since most of us pray less than we believe we should, we are impressed with long prayers. And in them our minds wander up and down those aisles of the chapel, keeping up a veritable juggling act of dis-tracted thoughts.

We may well find ourselves in Satan's chapel if we forget that our prayers for forgiveness must include mercy for those who have wronged us. We shut ourselves off from forgiveness if we refuse it to others. Satan's chapel is the only place open to the unjust steward who, saved from prison by the grace of his employer, threw the debtor who owed him a few cents into jail.

There, too, is the pray-er who prays "*My* will be done" rather than "*Thy* will be done," words that are unmistakably enshrined in the house of prayer. How wonderful to know that the Holy Spirit, the ever-present director/teacher in the house of prayer, conducts a twenty-four-hour foray into enemy territory to bring us back from Satan's chapel to the house of prayer. He enrolls us in his school of prayer and teaches us how to stay steadfastly in that place. Even the helpless plea for release from Satan's chapel is met by the Father's grace and answered by his abundance.

I long for your saving help, O Lord. Teach me how to live daily in your house of prayer. Amen.

Challenge: Write a paragraph description of your prayer life. Is there anything revealed to you that you need to be especially aware of and seek the Holy Spirit's guidance to correct?

More Money

"You cannot serve both God and money" (verse 13).

> *"Although they lived in style, they felt always an anxiety in the house. There was never enough money. The mother had a small income, and the father had a small income, but not nearly enough for the social position which they had to keep up....*
>
> *"And so the house came to be haunted by the unspoken phrase: There must be more money. There must be more money! The children could hear it all the time, though nobody said it aloud....Behind the shining modern rocking-horse, behind the smart doll's house, a voice would start whispering, "There must be more money! There **must** be more money!"*
>
> D. H. Lawrence, "The Rocking-Horse Winner"

Probably few of us know the degree to which our attitudes and even our decisions are affected by the voice that haunted the house in D. H. Lawrence's story: "There must be more money! There must be more money!" It was not that the family needed the money for food or shelter. "There must be more money!" There were style, social position, honor, status to be maintained. "There must be more money!" And the child, sensing what he cannot fully understand, focuses all his psychic powers on coming to know the name of the winning horse which will add money to the family treasury, and spurs his rocking-horse into the fever of death.

How would our decisions be different if other questions were more important than the boy's in our daily lives? With what kind of commitment do we handle the money we have? How does our use of it square with the concerns of the prophets that the poor, the voiceless and the powerless be cared for? I have just read an issue of *Prison Fellowship*, the publication of the organization begun by Charles Colson to work in prisons. How many of us have ever directed some of our "more money" to bring Good News to a single prisoner? Of course not all of us should. Some of us should be financing the hospices like Mother Teresa's in Calcutta; some of us should be paying for the digging of wells in Africa to bring water for thirsty people to drink and for hungry people to grow crops. Some of us should support Bible Societies that all may hear the Gospel.

Perhaps we should take the words the child in Lawrence's story hears from all over his parents' house and use them to remind God's people that in the face of the world's inequalities and injustices and lack of love "There must be more money. There *must* be more money!"

As the people of God who would be his hands in a needy world, we face a challenge to order our way of life so that there *is* more money for his hands to use. Then our activity will lead not to death but to life.

Lord, make mine a generous heart that more of those who hunger and thirst both spiritually and physically may be fed. Amen.

Challenge: Reread II Cor. 8, looking for its guidance in stewardship.

Generations

"The elders who do good work as leaders should be considered worthy of receiving double pay, especially those who work hard at preaching and teaching" (verse 17).

> Solness: (to Hilda) "I must tell you—I have be-
> gun to be so afraid—so terribly afraid of the younger
> generation....I tell you the younger generation will
> one day come and thunder at my door! They will
> break in upon me."
> Hilda: "Then I say you ought to go out and open
> the door to the younger generation."
>
> Henrik Ibsen, <u>The Master Builder</u>

Ibsen's "master builder," Halvard Solness, is a building contractor, skilled but unscrupulous, deliberately holding down the men under him that he might not have to deal with the competition they could be to him, either by their youth or their expertise. If they could get free from his control, either the architect or the draftsman could do better than he, but he makes sure they cannot. Into his life, far more attractive than his listless wife who has never been able to handle adult life, comes the daring, laughing, mountain girl Hilda, who challenges him to conquer his fear of heights by "topping" the roof of the new house he has built for himself.

Halvard knows his fear of high places, but there is another fear with which he struggles. He reaches out for Hilda's youth as though in her admiration for him he could prove his ability to compete with others of her generation. His guilty conscience tells him that "the younger generation will one day come and thunder at my door. They will break in on me."

Halvard is right. That day is soon to come. He cannot forever fend off their competition. And Hilda is right when she advises him to voluntarily open the door to the younger generation. Youth and age need to live cooperatively, each supplying what a balanced society needs. Unfortunately, Halvard's ego is stronger than his good sense, and he dies trying to prove he is as brave as ever.

Paul, writing to his protege from the younger generation, Timothy, gives him sage advice about the relationship between the generations in the congregation where Timothy serves. The wisdom and experience of the elders are to be respected and rewarded.

We in our present society have much to learn in this matter—whether it be allowing more room for the younger generation knocking at the door or more respect for the older generation with its experience and wider outlook. There is pain when, for a variety of reasons, older workers who still have much to give are edged out before they are ready to retire. There is also anger and frustration when young workers can find no place in their careers because people who have already had a full career insist on remaining on the job as if they are indispensable. Halvard and Hilda both need to be listened to—and to listen to each other.

I long for your help, O Lord, to see the needs of all ages in perspective and have a respect for the capabilities of all. Amen.

Challenge: Examine carefully your own attitudes toward people of other age groups to see if you find any resentments or jealousies that need to be dealt with.

The Blessing of Work

"Whoever refuses to work is not allowed to eat" (verse 10).

> *"When men are employed, they are best contented; for on the days they worked they were good-natured and cheerful, and with the consciousness of having done a good day's work, they spend the evening jollily; but on our idle days they were mutinous and quarrelsome."*
>
> B. Franklin, <u>Autobiography</u>

Paul clearly attributes salvation to "grace through faith," but we notice he is not slow to give his spiritual children firm advice about how to live their daily lives in a way that is a credit to the Christian community. If they "talk the talk" they must also "walk the walk" convincingly to those outside that community.

One of the qualities Paul stresses is the willingness to work. There had been a problem in Thessalonica, where believers had been persuaded that Jesus would soon return. They had sold their belongings, quit their jobs, and settled back to wait for his appearance. Paul, hearing reports of this, has been in touch with the Thessalonian Christians. He has been quite firm in his remonstrance: "Whoever refuses to work is not allowed to eat." "We hear that there are some...who do nothing except meddle in other people's business."

Early Americans like Benjamin Franklin were in hearty agreement with St. Paul. Captain John Smith echoed Paul's ultimatum connecting working and eating. Franklin saw work as a psychological necessity. A frontier country has little patience with non-workers.

Work in our day has had a bad press. Affluence has made hard work less necessary for many people. An ever-growing type of economy in which money is earned by financial manipulation rather than by physical labor has created more leisure time. If work is tied to psychological well-being, what does that mean in the lives of our large number of unemployables? In the last two decades, many of our most dissatisfied youth have come from homes in which they have had little experience with work. Is there a relationship there?

Biblical wisdom writings show great respect for work. "No matter how much a lazy person may want something, he will never get it. A hard worker will get everything he wants" (Prov. 13:4). Perhaps. We may be slower today to accept at face value the relation between hard work and prosperity, and surely we *should* be slow to determine the human value of an individual by the physical exertion of which he is capable. But there is sturdy Christian common sense in respecting the worth of honest work—physical, mental, spiritual. It may keep us as well as the Thessalonians from being "mutinous and quarrelsome."

I long for your help, O Lord, in appreciating the work that is mine to do. May I do it well to glorify you. Remind us to continue to honor those who have retired from long years of labor. Amen.

Challenge: Be grateful for the most exhausting work you have to do. If you are physically an invalid, work on being a spiritual athlete.

Strange Choices

"And so I tell you, Peter: You are a rock, and on this rock foundation I will build my church" (verse 18).

"Yet such is oft the course of deeds that move the wheels of the world: small hands do them because they must, while the eyes of the great are elsewhere."
J. R. R. Tolkien
Lord of the Rings: The Fellowship of the Ring

Who but God, when a great church leader was needed, would pick a rustic fisherman? Or who but God, when he needed a missionary to India's hungry millions, would have called a shoemaker from his bench and his tools? God seems to have the strangest taste in his choice of people! Or so we say.

Some years ago my students often seemed to be talking about J. R. R. Tolkien's *The Lord of the Rings.* Again and again they asked me if I had read it yet. No, I hadn't. Again, haven't you read it *yet*? Finally, I capitulated. I read it during the day, finding that its depiction of evil left me sleepless if I tried to read it at night. The characters came into clear focus—Gandalf, the wizard, a great candidate to be lord of the rings. Or was it Aragorn, the king to come—tall, handsome, regal? Or Legolas the elf, tall, willowy, loyal, and fair? The elves had special powers; surely Legolas was lordly. But to my delight, it was soon evident that the approved one to be hero, the chosen one to save Middle-Earth from the corrupt power of the Dark Lord, was none of these, impressive though they might be, but instead the humble furry hobbit, Frodo. Whoever would have guessed it— despite the many authors through the centuries who have used the common plot of the unexpected and the unsung hero. Frodo's hobbit-feet carry him painfully to the Crack of Doom where he may throw to its destruction the ring sought by the forces of evil. The "small hands" do the deeds "because they must, while the eyes of the great are elsewhere."

What deeds are there for our "small hands" to do for the Kingdom? Is there some evil influence that needs to be fought in our community? Or can we be the loyal and supportive Sam Gamgee without whom Frodo could never have won the victory? We may never be either Frodo or the Apostle Peter. But the power did not lie with Peter. It lay with the Lord whom Peter confessed. That Lord gave Peter the title of "the Rock" and used him to build his church. That Lord used William Carey and Martin Luther King—Senior and Junior, and the one through whose care you were brought to Christ. On and on the list goes. Let the eyes of the great be on power and prestige and glory. In the power of Christ we are sufficient for what needs to be done.

Lord, there is not much power in my hands until you cover them with your own, and cause them to move for your glory. I long for your help to do what I need to do in the place where I live. Amen.

Challenge: What evil influence in your community needs to be resisted wisely and patiently? Volunteer your help in the struggle against it.

All or Nothing

"I know that you are neither cold nor hot. How I wish you were either one or the other" (verse 15).

"To every man there openeth
A Way, and Ways, and a Way,
The High Soul climbs the High Way,
The Low Soul gropes the Low,
And in between, on the misty flats,
The rest drift to and fro."
                    John Oxenham, "The Ways"

I know people who deliberately drink hot water and say they like it. Many of us fret if the water we drink is not ice cold. I don't think I have ever heard anyone express enthusiasm for a drink of lukewarm water. Christ, "the Amen, the faithful and true witness" who assesses the state of the Laodecian church, also rejects the lukewarm, the wobbling indecisive thing that is neither one thing or the other, neither hot nor cold.

Dante in his *Inferno* reserves one of the areas of Hell for those who were neither good nor evil in this life, who were so indecisive that they were on neither side. There they hung swaying one way and the other in eternal vacillation. A historian of one of the ancient Greek city states records that in the case of civil mutiny the winners were rewarded, the losers penalized, but those who had stood on the sidelines without taking sides were executed: they of all were most contempt-ible.

When Elijah challenged the priests of Baal to see whose God could call down fire to consume the offer-ings, their lack of conviction, their unwillingness to live by their beliefs was his charge. "How much longer will it take you to make up your minds? If the Lord is God, worship him; but if Baal is God, worship him!" (I Kings 18:21). His challenge went unanswered.

In a day in which we pride ourselves on our tolerance, in acceptance of pluralistic open-mindedness, how easy it is to be comfortable in lukewarmness. Enthusiasm among us is reserved for the young who haven't been cooled by experience, or assigned to certain types of personalities, at which we smile a bit condescendingly. "All or nothing" may be impressive in Ibsen's character Brand, but only in theory would we consent to be pinned down to that degree of commitment to our faith. Most of us would prefer to remain "In between, on the misty flats" of moderation.

One of the uncomfortable but compelling aspects of Paul is the totality of his commitment. He is fully dedicated to his task of persecuting the believers. All the way! But when that fiery enthusiasm encounters the bright light of faith, that great "all or nothing" of Paul's commitment is used to expand the Christian church and establish the believers.

Is life so long that we can go limping between two sides, can cool down the warmth of God's love before we share it with others? Jesus warns, "Because you are lukewarm, neither hot nor cold, I am going to spit you out of my mouth." The "misty flats" are not fertile ground for our life in Christ.

I long for your saving help, O Lord, to give me courage and commitment to choose sides and order my life accordingly. Amen.

Challenge: Before this time tomorrow, witness verbally to your faith in Christ to someone with whom you speak.

In Need of Praise

"...the tax collector, and not the Pharisee, was in the right with God when he went home" (verse 14).

"Two went to pray? Oh, rather say
One went to brag, the other to pray;
One stands up close and treads on high
Where the other dares not send his eye;
One nearer to God's altar trod,
The other to the altar's God.

Richard Crashaw
"Two Went Up to the Temple to Pray"

Different as their attitudes were, the Pharisee and the tax collector went to the temple for the same commendable reason. Both felt the desire to pray, and both knew where God had promised to meet those who would seek him. Both had something they wanted to say to God. And there the similarity between the two ends.

The Pharisee, deliberately separating himself from others—even other Pharisees—no doubt raised his eyes and held up his arms in the proper stance for prayer. He had been taught, at least by the example of the psalmists, that prayer should begin with thanksgiving. But it is rather hard to give thanks if all one wants to talk about is oneself, no? Perhaps he is a little abashed to say "I thank you, God, that I am generous, honest, and morally pure—as other people are not." If he dare not claim those positive qualities, at least he need not plead guilty to the negative ones of greed, dishonesty or adultery. And surely he can safely claim not to be like that despised tax collector off on the fringes of the temple crowd. Why did the temple guard ever let him come inside?

In the days of Jesus, devout Pharisees usually fasted Mondays and Thursdays. The one in our story assures God he does his full duty in fasting, and gives his tithe—evidently on his gross income. His prayer ends very abruptly. There is nothing he wants to ask of God; he is only making a status report. His thanks is not for what God is, but praise for what he himself is. What more does he need from God? Only attention to his self-praise.

Perhaps this self-righteous man was hungry for the praise of others and got little of it. Those who in total self-absorption wait for the praises of others are often abrasive and super-critical of others, unwilling to give those around them the space to live. Because others refuse to feed their need for ego-reinforcement, they must sound their own praises, unable to understand why they are left standing by themselves.

The Pharisee goes home from his errand to the temple unsatisfied and unfulfilled. The "tax collector, and not the Pharisee, was in the right with God when he went home." Sadly, the Pharisee probably didn't even know why.

Lord, there is so much of the Pharisee in me. I would love to tell you, if I dared, all my good qualities which deserve praise. I long for your saving love to help me understand how threadbare my list of virtues is. Amen.

Challenge: Each of us develops a way of handling our need for praise. Some ways are helpful, others negative. Take a few minutes to think through your personal method and evaluate it. Thank God for those who help you satisfy that need in a healthy way.

Big and Little Thieves

"If then you have not been faithful in handling worldly wealth, how can you be trusted with true wealth?" (verse 11).

"For de little stealin' dey gits you in jail soon or late. For de big stealin' dey makes you emperor and puts you in de Hall o' Fame when you croakes. If dey's one thing I learns in ten years on de Pullman cars listening' to de white quality talk, it's dat same fact."

Eugene O'Neill, <u>The Emperor Jones</u>

Jesus' advice on financial matters brought laughter from the Pharisees who heard him speak. One can imagine the rapidity with which their smiles turned to angry scowls at Jesus' response. "You are the ones who make yourselves look right in other people's sight, but God knows your hearts." O'Neill's Emperor Jones would understand that statement. He had observed the flip-flop of human judgments applied to rich and poor in society, to white-collar crime as compared to the "little stealing" for which the poor are readily imprisoned. An objective study of the equality of justice meted out to those involved in little and big stealing in our land—and others—would not make comfortable reading.

Some of Jesus' statements about the use of money are difficult to understand, as they are in the above text. Jesus, for instance, commends the behavior of the shrewd steward who uses his authority to win himself friends among his employer's debtors, and tells his listeners that the "people of this world are more shrewd in handling their affairs than the people who belong to the light."

Much in this text is unclear to me, but I do understand that God expects me as his follower to use intelligent stewardship in handling my finances. True, they are not as important in the long run as spiritual values, but "If, then, you have not been faithful in handling worldly wealth, how can you be trusted with true wealth?" I cannot serve both God and money, but I can, with attention and care, learn to use my money to serve God. The Kingdom has been furthered by those who have sacrificially given the widow's mite; it has also been furthered by those who have wisely invested and saved this world's wealth in order that it may be capital from which Kingdom activities may be established.

Jesus implies that God watches, not the money itself but the values that are revealed by its use. As with other aspects of my life, it is the commitment and love directed to God as the Master of my life that is the touchstone. I cannot serve money, but I can use money in grateful service of God. That money must come from honest business, done in the sight of him who judges honestly between the "little stealing" and the "big stealing" which in his eyes are both wrong.

Lord, help me to use sanctified common sense to handle rightly and profitably that which you have given me for Kingdom purposes. Amen.

Challenge: Make a practice of reading a financial magazine or newspaper to make yourself more knowledgeable about how to use your money wisely.

Walking on Water

*"Lord, if it is really you, order me to come out on the
water to you" (verse 28).*

"Yea, in the night, my Soul, my daughter,
Cry,—clinging Heaven by the horns
And lo, Christ walking on the water
Not of Gennesareth, but Thames!
　　　　Francis Thompson, "The Kingdom of God"

Peter can hardly believe his eyes, even though in
the miraculous breaking of bread earlier that day he
had already seen the power of God in the acts of Jesus.
But in the meantime Peter's seaman-mind has been
occupied with the turbulent wind and water. He is not
the only one of the disciples to have trouble with recog-
nizing the Master in the darkness and the storm. Like
the others, he has no doubt cried out with fear. Even the
reassuring voice of Jesus is hardly enough to persuade
Peter of the Lord's identity. If it is really the Lord, let
there be another miracle and Peter will have faith.
"Lord,...order me to come out on the water to you."
And at Jesus' invitation, the fisherman, who all his life
has known the Sea of Galilee, gets out of the boat and
walks toward Jesus. As long as his eyes are on the Lord,
the water is firm under his feet. But when he looks at the
sea blown by the wind, that is another matter.

This walking on the water of the Sea of Galilee, is it
a one-time experience among believers? In the lines
from Thompson's poem, he clearly says no. The waters
of the Thames also have known that step. Along its
banks, General William Booth has led forth an army of
outcasts, unwelcome in the churches of their day, dedicated to spreading the Good News. Peter is not the only

one who in faith has walked upon the water, has risen at Christ's command to do what humans have called impossible.

Francis Thompson knew something about that command firsthand. A victim of opium addiction, Thompson, through the loving aid of a Christian couple, heard the command of Jesus to "Come," and walked to victory over his addiction.

Martin Luther, wrestling over the sufficiency of good works for salvation, heard that "Come" and walked out on the waters to preach the message of the faith that saves.

Martin Luther King, Jr., longing to help set his people free from prejudice and discrimination, heard the words and led out in faith that "We shall overcome."

Charles Colson, ambitious and willing to bend the right to get to the top, heard the "Come" and walked across the waters of suspicion and jeering to establish a ministry for those who society said would never rise above the morass of crime.

Corrie ten Boom heard that "Come" among the horrors of the concentration camp and walked out to demonstrate the power to forgive one's enemies.

Everyone knows you cannot walk on water—everyone, that is, except those who have answered the command to "Come" and gone on to do the impossible at the Spirit's enabling.

I long for your saving help, O Lord, to be more able to believe that the humanly impossible may at your command be the divinely possible. Amen.

Challenge: What that you have really longed to do in the Kingdom have you left undone because you thought it impossible to do by human strength? Talk it over with the Lord and see if he says "Come."

John 9:1

That Which is Mine to Do

"As long as it is day, we must do the work of him who sent me; night is coming when no one can work" (verse 4).

"...yet it is not our part to master all the tides of the world, but to do what is in us for the succour of those years wherein we are set, uprooting the evil in the fields that we know, so that those who live after may have clean fields to till. What weather they shall have is not ours to rule."

Tolkien
Lord of the Ring: Return of the King

One of the delights of J. R. R. Tolkien's *The Lord of the Rings* for the adult reader is the presence of well-expressed and convincing wisdom, of which we all need reminders. Often it comes through the words of Gandalf, the prophet/wise man; sometimes through the words of Aragorn, the king-to-come, and also through the words of the little hobbit Frodo, the suffering servant who takes on himself the challenge of destroying the evil that threatens not only his shire but all the world known to hobbits and humans. (Prophet, king-to-come, suffering servant—do you find these images familiar?)

Gandalf's words in this quotation touch a truth it is easy to forget. How easy to feel that because we cannot do *all* that needs to be done, there is no way to do anything! With millions of children starving, what can I do that will make the problem of scarcity significantly less crucial? With violence so frighteningly ever-present in our society, what meaningful opposition to it can I generate? What can I do about the evils of apartheid in South Africa or bigotry in Podunk Corners, U.S.A.?

What good does my simplifying my lifestyle do in preserving earth's resources? In the "brave new world" of the next century's mind-conditioning, what does my struggle to retain the worth of the individual accomplish?

Gandalf's words speak to those concerns: we need not seek to struggle against all evils at once. We need not expect to conquer all evils in our generation, but *to do what is in us* in our lifetime to make a better life for those in the generation that follows. We need not take on all worlds; we clean the fields which we know. Then they can bear fruit for those who follow in the "weather" that is theirs.

If I cannot stop famine in Africa, I can share some of my money with others to dig a well to bring clean water to an African village. I can seek to be informed about the platforms of those for whom I vote so that I do not strengthen the hands of those who seek to pour billions into overkill. I cannot do everything, but I can do something—and I can quit countenancing my own excuses for doing so little. Surely it should not be hard to see in our time that "As long as it is day we must do the work of him who sent me; night is coming when no one can work." There is something that is ours to do.

Lord, I long for your saving help, to uproot the evil in the fields that I know so that those who come after me may have cleaner fields to till. In Jesus' name, Amen.

Challenge: If you have not already done so, choose one social evil about which you feel strongly and do something this week to involve yourself in the struggle against it.

Keep Running

"Run your best in the race of faith,..." (verse 12).

> *"If this life be not a real fight, in which something is eternally gained for the universe by success, it is no better than a game of private theatricals from which one may withdraw at will. But it **feels** like a real fight."*
>
> William James, "The Will to Believe"

As I sit by my window writing—it is early morning—there is an unsteady stream of people, mostly university students, jogging or running by. Some have shoulders erect, elbows tucked in, chin up, and expressions of satisfaction. Others are obviously winded, have poor form, and pained expressions. Some are too exhausted to even greet other runners; others are able to carry on conversations with their companions. Many are dressed for jogging but have slowed to a walk. Others will obviously reach the residence halls not even out of breath. For many it is obvious that these final blocks are a real fight—a fight between the will and a tired body.

Paul often drew on the metaphor of the race in his description of the Christian life. "Run your best in the race of faith." "Surely you know that many runners take part in a race, but only one of them wins a prize"; "I run straight for the finish line"; "I harden my body...and bring it under control" (I Cor. 9:24, 26, 27). The author of Hebrews uses the same metaphor. "So then, let us rid ourselves of everything that gets in the way, and of the sin which holds on to us so tightly, and let us run with determination the race that lies before us" (Heb. 12:1).

Many joggers and other runners take their activity with great seriousness—as William James takes life as a real struggle. "It *feels* like a real fight." The metaphor of battle is another frequently used by Paul. "I am like a boxer who does not waste my punches," he writes to the Corinthians. "Fight the worthwhile battle of the faith. Keep your grip on that life eternal to which you have been called, and to which you boldly professed your loyalty before many witnesses" (I Tim. 6:12).

Certainly our lives as God's people are no "game of private theatricals from which one may withdraw at will." We "are not fighting against human beings but against the wicked spiritual forces in the heavenly world, the rulers, authorities, and cosmic powers of this dark age" (Eph. 6:12). And that, as one radio commentator says, is "something to think about."

I long for your empowering help, O Lord, to fight the good fight of the faith, knowing that victory is possible in your strength. Amen.

Challenge: Take a brisk, vigorous walk today. While you are doing so, look for similarities between your walk and "running your best in the race of faith."

The Risk of Love

"Whoever accepts my commandments and obeys them is the one who loves me" (verse 21).

"Yes, that is right about power, he said. But there is only one thing that has power completely, and that is love. Because when a man loves, he seeks no power, and therefore he has power. I see only one hope for our country, and that is when white men and black men, desiring neither power nor money, but desiring only the good of their country, come together to work for it.

"He [Msimangu] was grave and silent, and then he said sombrely, I have one great fear in my heart, that one day when they are turned to loving, they will find we are turned to hating."

Alan Paton, <u>Cry, the Beloved Country</u>

Two of the most beautiful characters in all fiction are Stephen Kumalo, the Zulu country pastor of *Cry, the Beloved Country*, and his city friend Msimangu. Kumalo searches heartbrokenly for his son in Johannesburg. Msimangu, knowing the city and how many young men it has corrupted, yearns to help. They seek aid from Kumalo's brother John, who has turned against the religion of his brother and seeks power in political demagoguery. But there is neither love nor pity in him, and the two pastors turn away disheartened and sickened by his lack of caring. His kind of power will never make men free.

Msimangu, like Arthur Jarvis, the Lincoln-like white man who has been killed by Kumalo's son in a burglary attempt, believes that only in love is there power to change either the human heart or South Africa. Love—

perfect love—casts out fear, the fear that causes us to build walls around ourselves to shut others out. If only that love can grow in time, before hate can have its way! For Kumalo's son it is too late. Perhaps his unborn child and the little son of Jarvis can in their generation love each other.

In a society in which crime against the person increases year by year, how many of us see in extending the power of love the answer to the crime problem? Study after study informs us that imprisonment corrupts rather than reforms. Yet the proposals for "solving" the crime problem almost inevitably are for building larger, more, and more secure prisons.

We talk much about love in the church, that body of those who know their need of the love of God. But do we really believe that love has power to change? Are we willing to begin to love those we fear, to begin soon enough so that we will not find when we have belatedly begun to love that we meet only implacable hate from those who feared us? Love takes risks. A lover is always vulnerable. Yet it is that willingness to step out on the power of love that is the obedience that God calls for. He has taken the risk of our rebuff in loving us. Now he calls us to take the risk of loving others for whom he died. If we are rebuffed, shall the servant be greater than the Master?

Loving Father and Lord, I find it easy to love the majority of those about me. I long for your saving help to love those I find it hard even to tolerate. Amen.

Challenge: Who is the least likable person you know in your block or apartment building? Make one specific move to be friendly to that person today. (Surprisingly, a good way is to ask a favor of that person.)

God's Wisdom or Ours?

"For what seems to be God's foolishness is wiser than human wisdom, and what seems to be God's weakness is stronger than human strength" (verse 25).

"By all ye cry or whisper,...
The silent sullen peoples
Shall weigh your God and you."

Rudyard Kipling
"The White Man's Burden"

What incredibly strange priorities we humans tend to set in the ordering of our lives! And because we individual believers make up the church, which is in part an earthly body, what strange priorities the Church sometimes sets! Paul already knew that well. "The foolishness of God is wiser than the wisdom of men," he observed.

Surely it is true that what seems to be important to one may be trivia in the estimation of another. It is more important to be "sensible" than to be sacrificial in our love for others—isn't it? Jesus surely did not mean what he said when he advised us to turn the other cheek rather than to retaliate, did he? The great majority of church people do not believe that he did (if they did, no government could get away with spending billions of dollars for military overkill). It is important to admire someone so perfect as Jesus, but to be like him? He never made it into the power structure of his day, did he? He was involved instead in that scandal of the cross, wasn't he? Scandal and disgrace are low on our list of priorities, though we have to admire some who choose to follow Jesus through scandal and disgrace.

But it isn't for us—right? What would people around us think?

If Jesus in the flesh were coming to our town next Wednesday, how would we prepare? The ministerium might suggest the largest church in town to hold those who would like to see him. A mass choir in the welcoming service—and the most ornate silver services around for the reception, no doubt. The biggest parking lot, of course. I believe we can put all those plans away. The "foolishness of the cross" would let our coffee grow cold while Jesus spent his time with the humblest and the poorest and the most neglected and least lovely.

We really find it very difficult, don't we, to get through our heads that we cannot follow Jesus and put first on our list of priorities our own social status and security and our reputation for being level-headed, wise leaders in a stable, prosperous church. God isn't counting up our memberships on the committees that carry with them the prestige in town. The God who sent his son to die on a cross for humans who had rejected and reviled his way of love is not a "sensible" God, is he? His prodigal love is as much higher than our ideas of what is desirable as our championing the despised and voiceless in our society is higher than our spending our time getting to know the "right" people in town.

If we ever really caught the vision of what following Jesus' pattern of behavior means, there would not only be a revolution in town. There would be one in every church in town.

O Lord, I long for your help to develop the bravery I need to begin to pay attention to your definition of wisdom rather than my own. Amen.

Challenge: Read I Corinthians 1-4. Paul is a church leader fighting for his right to lead. Notice what his priorities are.

Living Recklessly

"Remember that the person who plants few seeds will have a small crop; the one who plants many seeds will have a large crop" (verse 6).

"Let us be reckless of our words and worlds,
And spend them freely as the tree his leaves;..."
                                        Conrad Aiken
                                "One Star Fell and Another"

Being cautious comes so naturally to us, especially as we grow older. Our time, our resources, our talents—we let them go from us so sparingly, so fearful that we will never have that supply again. And that, of course, is true. The talent—whether it be for friendship, for art, for song—hidden cautiously away never produces a large crop. The money hoarded carefully away earns no interest, let alone gratitude. The time saved so stingily for our own rest, spent so reluctantly in the Kingdom, speeds on, leaving us yawning in our boredom.

There is a kind of heavenly recklessness recommended both by our Scripture verse and Aiken's poem. The author of Ecclesiastes warns: "If you wait until the wind and the weather are just right, you will never plant anything and never harvest anything" (11:4). We recognize the truth on a temporal level. The one who has saved his crop from a night of frost is left to grieve over crop failure from drought; the one who has waited for the perfect day to plant may find his seed molding in the soggy ground of a rainy spell. The talent hidden in the ground draws no interest.

In the spiritual realm this lesson is even more true. The gifts the Spirit of God portions to us are not given in niggardly measure for cautious use. The love He pours through us is not diminished by being shared: it multiplies. The reservoir of grace has sprung no leak; it brims when grace is drawn upon and rejoiced in. "Whoever shares with others should do it generously; whoever has authority should work hard; whoever shows kindness to others should do it cheerfully" (Rom. 12:8). God challenges us to a holy recklessness!

Lord of love and generosity, we long for your help to set us free from stinginess and overdone self-protectiveness. May we turn what is ours free in sanctified extravagance, knowing that you will never be in any person's debt. In the name of our Lord who gave all. Amen.

Challenge: Read Malachi, especially Chapter 3. How does it relate to our meditation?

Waters Rushing Back

*"Well, then," Jesus said, "I do not condemn you
either. Go, but do not sin again" (verse 11).*

*"at the time i dropped your almost body down...
what did i know about waters rushing back...."*
    Lucille Clifton, "The Lost Baby Poem"

The fact that the baby to be born to the woman who
speaks in Lucille Clifton's poem would have arrived in
the "winter of no car" and unaffordable heat does not
stop the mother of that "almost body" from experienc-
ing the waters of memory and guilt rushing back over
her. The tiny aborted fetus she has flushed down to
"run on with the sewage to the sea" is still present in her
consciousness, and she tries futilely to explain to the
baby who is gone how she hadn't been able to stand the
thought of letting it go into stranger's hands. With this
terrible sense of guilt hanging over her, she vows that
she will be a "mountain" for her other "definite" children or else deserve only the condemnation of her
people. The poem is a gripping one that has no doubt
encapsulated the emotions of unknown numbers of
women.

We do not know the inner feelings of the woman
brought to Jesus at a time in her life when taunts and
shame were heaped upon her. There was no question
that she had offended the law—but no more than many
of those who flung her before the Savior and demanded
her stoning. Puzzling them by his behavior, Jesus
stooped to write on the ground. "Whichever one of you
has committed no sin may throw the first stone at her."
One by one they left, the older ones first (perhaps time
does teach us some humility after all), knowing some-

thing of those "waters rushing back" about which Clifton wrote. Where, in this scene, is the man with whom she was found? If she is guilty, is he less so?

Those who sought to accuse the woman were really wanting to accuse Jesus. Are there times when we who are so quick to accuse others really are seeking to show our resentment of the moral pattern Jesus' sinless life places before us? His forgiveness falls on us, as it fell on the woman, like a beautiful benediction, and with it comes his voice reminding us, "Go, but do not sin again." Forgiveness is not ours that we may be free to return to the evil that attracts us; it comes to release us from the desire to sin again. "Do not judge others, and God will not judge you; do not condemn others, and God will not condemn you; forgive others and God will forgive you. Give to others, and God will give to you. Indeed, you will receive a good measure, a generous helping, poured into your hands—all that you can hold" (Lk. 8:37-38).

Lord, make me more quick to forgive than to condemn, to see the sin in myself rather than to point it out in others. Amen.

Challenge: Is there someone you have been omitting from your company because of the kind of life he or she has lived? Do something today to draw them back into your circle.

Dilemma

"I have never trusted in riches or taken pride in my wealth" (verses 24-25).

"The truth is that our Christian civilization is riddled through and through with dilemma....We believe in help for the underdog, but we want him to stay under....The truth is that our civilization is not Christian; it is a tragic compound of great ideal and fearful practice, of high assurance and desperate anxiety, of loving charity and fearful clutching of possessions. Allow me a minute...."
Alan Paton, <u>Cry the Beloved Country</u>

Job makes a striking statement as he puts together the brief for his audience with God—if only he can have one. He makes a claim which many of us in our affluent society could not make. "I have never trusted in riches or taken pride in my wealth." Perhaps that is the reason he could lose his wealth and say, "The Lord gave, and now he has taken away. May his name be praised!" (Job 1:21).

Many centuries later, the South African writer Alan Paton looks at modern society and finds, as we would, a very different attitude among people who, if honest, would have to say, "I have firm trust in my riches and take pride in my wealth." He concludes that our civilization is *not* Christian. The young Jarvis, who is Paton's mouthpiece in *Cry the Beloved Country*, says in his manuscript for a speech that our civilization is a "tragic compound of great ideals and fearful practice,...of loving charity and fearful clutching of possessions." Then, hearing a noise below, he goes to meet his death at the hands of a burglar.

Perhaps there are a few countries—small and homogeneous—that can accurately be called Christian. In many others, Christianity is a force to be reckoned with, weak or strong. Most countries today, in the western world at least, are pluralistic. Government and society are supposedly so designed as to protect the rights of minorities. Even aside from that, we can hardly claim that we are a Christian society. Yes, we have great ideals, not consistently honored in practice. We speak with great assurance—and take tranquilizers by the million to handle our anxieties. We all too often volunteer help for the underdog only so long as he will remain one. Have we really changed our values since the suicide statistics for the Stock Market crash of 1929 were printed?

Are we really so different from the people of Old Testament times who judged a person's righteousness by his prosperity? For what blessings are we first thankful? We should be thankful for material blessings, but should they come first? Our civilization will be truly Christian when we reveal a compound of great ideal and *confident* practice, of high assurance and low anxiety, of loving clarity and *generous sharing* of possessions.

I long for your saving help, O Lord, to make my attitudes toward my possessions like those of Job. Amen.

Challenge: Go back through your income tax forms and compare the percentage of your income that went to benevolences last year to that which you gave five years ago.

A Reason for Discomfort

"When you give a feast, invite the poor, the crippled, the lame, and the blind, and you will be blessed...." (verse 13).

"A decent provision for the poor is the true test of civilization."
Samuel Johnson, in Boswell's *Life of Johnson*

Peter Marshall, in one of his sermons in *Mr. Jones, Meet the Master,* portrays a large dwelling from which the limousines go out to gather for a banquet the bums from Skid Row, the destitutes who are crippled and blind and who would never have expected to be invited. Someone was obeying the command of Jesus to extend one's hospitality, not to those who will repay it in like manner, but to those who can never repay.

The care of the poor is one of the most frequent—and most uncomfortable—concerns in the Bible. The laws of Torah safeguard the poor. The prophets thunder their denunciations of the affluent who are rich at the expense of the poor. Jesus ministers to them even while he admits the persistence of poverty—"The poor you have always with you." The disciples create deacons in the early church to assure that the poor are cared for. Paul gathers offerings in one congregation that the poor of another may be fed. Scripture is salted with admonitions to care for those who are poor, who can give nothing in return.

In our day the media have taken the place of Amos and Micah in insisting that we see the bloated bodies of starving children in the arms of grieving mothers—usually at the same time as we eat our too-heavily caloried evening meals. We at times feel almost put-upon by the inescapable insistence that we recognize our plenty in the face of the world's want. Some people refuse the pressure to share by insisting the poor are at fault for their own condition. One has to try hard if one is to make a starving baby responsible for its own plight. Some feel justified if they themselves were once poor. We feel frustrated by the vastness of the problem, cynical about whether the aid reaches the most needy, unsure what methods of aid are best. We listen to advocates of the "lifeboat theory" extol the necessity of letting starvation reduce the population of our planet to manageable proportions.

Uncomfortable as the problems of hunger and poverty make us, the words of Scripture are clear: "God chose the poor people of this world to be rich in faith....But you dishonor the poor!" (Jas. 2:5-6). The test for the rich young ruler, if he would follow Jesus, was to give all he had to the poor. Zacchaeus, his priorities rearranged by his encounter with Jesus, volunteered to give half of his goods to the poor.

Determining what is right to keep for oneself in the face of the poverty of others is one of our toughest personal moral problems as Christians. Earth's civilization is not doing too well with that "decent provision for the poor" that is its acid test.

Lord, grant me your saving help to know not only what I should give to the poor, but what it is right to keep for myself. Amen.

Challenge: What, by wiser buying and preparing, can you add to that which you set aside to help to feed the poor each month?

Monkey Ropes

"Help carry one another's burdens, and in this way you will obey the law of Christ" (verse 1).

"...Just so...did I hold Queequeg down there in the sea by what is called a monkey-rope....It must be said that the monkey-rope was fast at both ends; fast to Queequeg's broad canvas belt, and fast to my narrow leather one. So that for better or worse, we two, for the time, were wedded; and should poor Queequeg sink to rise no more, then both usage and honor demanded that instead of cutting the cord, it should drag me down in his wake....I saw that this situation of mine was the precise situation of every mortal that breathes;..."

Herman Melville, <u>Moby Dick</u>

Ishmael, a sailor on the ill-fated whaling ship in Melville's *Moby Dick*, explains above the arrangement that assures the safety of the man who is lowered on to the carcass of the dead whale drawn up alongside the ship. Ishmael, on deck, must keep Queequeg from being crushed between the ship and the body of the whale. If he fails to do that, honor demands that he let himself be pulled by Queequeg's struggle from the deck down into the fatal maelstrom. Just so, says Ishmael, is every human being linked with a multitude of others. "If your banker breaks, you snap; if your apothecary by mistake sends you poison in your pills, you die."

Paul, in the final chapter of his letter to the Galatians, tells the believers scattered throughout Galatia of the need to take on the risks and challenges of helping others to carry their burdens. So Christ commanded, and so we are to obey. It may not be very often that our responsibility is so frighteningly laid out as was Ishmael's for Queequeg. Yet we know, if we think about the matter at all, that our well-being, our safety, our health, and even our lives are in the hands of others—doctors, the drivers about us, a lawyer, those who prepare our food.

But what does Paul mean when by verse 5 he seems to have completely changed his mind? Rather than acknowledging the need to share the burdens of others, he says, "For everyone has to carry his own load." How do we reconcile what seems direct contradiction? If Queequeg down on the whale must care for himself, why must Ishmael share that danger? If I must carry my own load how should another be urged to help me with it?

Can we really be of much help to others unless we have at least made some progress in learning to bear our own burden? Perhaps Paul would say that unless Queequeg down on that slippery whale has some competence and confidence in what he is doing, having Ishmael bound to him will only result in the death of both. Paul then is saying we have a double responsibility: to let God work in us the strength to bear our own load of what life gives us, and beyond that to let him work through us to share the burden of others. How good to know that God's supply of strength is inexhaustible!

I long for your saving help, O Lord, to enable me both to handle my own "load" competently and to have strength left to share the burdens of those within the boundaries of my daily walk. Amen.

Challenge: We hear much about the importance of physical exercise. Look at your life to see what in it is the spiritual counterpart to physical conditioning.

In or Out of the Storm

"He helps us in all our troubles, so that we are able to help others who have all kinds of troubles,…" (verse 4).

And I have asked to be
Where no storms come,
Gerard Manley Hopkins, "Heaven Haven"

This brief poem by Hopkins has a sub-title in parenthesis—"A Nun Takes the Veil." Part of what has intrigued me about the poem since I first found it is the ambiguity that it suggests. The poet is an English Catholic priest from the early part of this century; the speaking voice is that of a nun. Each time I read it I wonder how Hopkins feels toward the desire of the nun for escape to a place where earth's problems cannot reach. He expresses her wishes so beautifully. Her experiences have made her aware of springs that fail as the Water of Life does not. Had she, perhaps, been caught away from shelter in a frightening hail storm? Flowers do not grow everywhere in the earth, but almost everywhere there is some kind of storm that churns the open sea into dangerous rolling swells against the protection of the harbor.

The images of safety and serenity the poet puts in the mouth of the nun are attractive to all of us. We, too, yearn for the unfailing springs and the quiet waters "out of the swing of the sea." We can understand her desire.

But are those valid reasons for her taking the veil? Will she find in the outward serenity of the convent the escape from the physical or psychological or even spiritual dangers she would like to have excluded from her

155

life? Is escape from the hurts and hard places of life the right motivation?

Is the desire for escape the right reason for us either? When we experience the joy of what Paul calls the "peace that passes understanding," is the right response "This is what I want to hide myself away in for the rest of my life"? The biographies of the saints and the spiritual leaders both of the past and the present suggest that is not the right response. God does not call us to the flowery meadows for all our days. He calls us to work and to battle and to serve—witness Mother Teresa with her ministry to the dying, or Dr. Paul Brand with his to the leper, and Stan Mooneyhan to the starving, or—the list could go on. Many of us do not live so dramatically in the storms and hail of personal sacrifice and suffering, but wherever we are it should not be our desire to escape but instead to minister to those who are in the storm and the hail and the drought, and to reach out to those caught in the swells of the sea of life. Not this earth but heaven is the haven that provides the perfect shelter. Even there, more than escape from trouble will be the reason for being.

Lord, thank you for shelter and rest from the storms of life, but I long for your help, not to mistakenly suppose that is all there is to serving you. Amen.

Challenge: Examine the balance in your life between escape and service, between rest and those things in which you engage in active encounter for others. Does there need to be some adjustment to make a better balance?

Enamored of God?

"Whoever does not love does not know God, for God is love" (verse 8).

"But Lily would not be put off. 'When,' she asked, in a trembly voice, 'did you become enamored of God?...'

"'I am not,' he said gravely, 'a talented religious person....I think,' he said in a strained manner, 'that I came to God not because I love Him, but because I did not.'"

Bernard Malamud, "The Magic Barrel"

Leo, the young rabbinical student in Malamud's story, has been struggling to choose between the old "matchmaker" method of seeking a wife and the modern American way of two young people finding each other. Finally he has called in the matchmaker, who has brought about the interview between Leo, soon to complete his preparation to be a rabbi, and Lily, who is obviously older than the matchmaker has said but who is deeply impressed with the idea of being married to a rabbi, to one who is close to God. When, she wants to know, did he become "enamored of God"?

Leo finds her question a difficult one—as we likely would too. Enamored of God? *Amour*—the word for love. Inflamed with love? Is that how we would describe our feelings for God? Leo cannot honestly say that is how he feels. The truth, he finally admits, is that "I came to God not because I love Him, but because I did not."

It takes courage to be so honest. To her whose respect for Leo is great because he is to be a spiritual teacher of his people, to admit his lovelessness, to say openly that he did not love God—the God of Abraham, Isaac, and Jacob, and his father? Yet are there not times when, if we are honest, we must admit the same lovelessness? Such love does not arise easily in the human heart.

Leo finds in the events that lead to his discovery of one he loves against all common sense and logic that to love someone else—even someone rejected and condemned—is a necessary step along the way of coming to love God. And conversely, concern about coming to love God opens the door to love of another human being as well. In Leo's unthinking spontaneous love for the daughter the matchmaker has disowned and disinherited, he can have hope of coming to be "enamored of God." So, too, in that opening of ourselves to love others, we may find ourselves enamored of the God who in our unworthiness has loved us. Coming to him in despair and repentance because we do not love him, we may find almost to our surprise that we do.

Father, my own emotions are often so confusing and uncertain to me. I long for your saving help to change my unbelief to faith, to change my lovelessness to a deep abiding love for you. Amen.

Challenge: Spend fifteen minutes meditating privately on the subject of your love to God. When are you most aware of that love? When least so? Spend much of that time praising God for his love for you.

Inescapable Consequences

"But whoever hates his brother is in the darkness; he walks in it and does no know where he is going because the darkness has made him blind" (verse 11).

"Even hatred for baseness Distorts one's features."

Bertolt Brecht
"To Those Born Later"

Is hatred for evil a virtue? Or does even hatred for evil carry with it the inescapable consequences of hatred in general? Does hatred always lead the hater into darkness? Perhaps hatred is such a black subject that we avoid thinking much about it lest it cast its dark shadows over us. Was David spiritually stronger because he said "O Lord, how I hate those who hate you!"—or was that what caused him immediately to need to pray "Examine me, O God, and know my mind;... Find out if there is any evil in me"? (Ps. 139:21, 24).

The poet-dramatist Brecht, anti-Fascist, has no doubt that hate has its unavoidable consequences even if directed at evil forces. "Even hatred for baseness / Distorts one's features." Even anger for a justifiable reason makes for a "hoarse rasping voice." Yet as he thinks of his fellow-fighters against fascism he seems to wonder what they could do differently. They mean well; their ends are justifiable. They are concerned to prepare the soil for kindness, but they themselves can not be gentle. They can only hope that "those born later" will realize their motivation and not judge them harshly.

Most of us have less vicious objects than did Brecht for our hatred and less justification for feeling it. Some advocate letting hatred out, supposing it will dissipate by being vented. It is interesting to see how our Lord, in a situation in which he would have had every justification for feeling and expressing hatred against those who were abusing him, quietly and urgently prayed "Forgive them, Father. They don't know what they are doing." And we remember him not leniently, as Brecht requests, but with awe and breathless respect. What kind of One is this who can meet evil and cruelty and cursing with love and forgiveness? He will not lead us *into* darkness but *through* the darkness of Calvary and the grave to the light of eternal glory. The darkness could not make him blind. It can through his strength and mercy lead us with him into everlasting light. It is not ours to judge those whose hatred for baseness distorts their features. But our Lord teaches us a better way—and an eternal one.

We long for your help, our Lord of Calvary, to find better motivation for struggling against baseness and injustice than hatred. Amen.

Challenge: Think carefully through a situation in which you have considered hatred justified. Was that really true?

His Example of Love

"*But now I tell you: do not take revenge on someone who wrongs you*" *(verse 39).*

> [The inquisitor] "*I turned back and joined the ranks of those* **who have corrected Thy work**....*I repeat, tomorrow Thou shalt see that obedient flock who at a sign from me will hasten to heap up the hot cinders about the pile on which I shall burn Thee for coming to hinder us. For if anyone has deserved our fires, it is Thou. Tomorrow I shall burn Thee, Dixi.*"
>
> Fyodor Dostoevsky
> "The Grand Inquisitor," <u>The Brothers Karamazov</u>

Perhaps most of us at some time or other have wondered what kind of welcome Jesus would receive if he should appear walking the streets of today's world, doing the kind of things he did when here two thousand years ago. Would we be any more ready to welcome him? Would either religious leaders with prestige and power or the mass of nominal Christians be any more ready to admit to the radical demands he makes on those who follow him?

One of the characters of Dostoevsky's *The Brothers Karamazov*, Ivan, the intellectual, tells his brother Aloysha, the monk, a fictional story of the grand inquisitor of Seville in the Spanish Inquisition. To the steps of the great cathedral of Seville one day comes One whom everyone recognizes instinctively, and before him they bow in worship when he gives life to a dead child. The great officer of the Inquisition comes upon the scene and immediately orders Jesus to be imprisoned. The next day he visits Christ in prison, complaining that this modern appearance was not in the agreement between Jesus and his church. The building of the Kingdom was left, the prelate says, in the hands of the hierarchy. Jesus just does not understand that human beings do not want the freedom Jesus speaks of. Instead they want bread (security), miracle, and mystery.

Jesus has no business, the inquisitor says, spoiling their plans when they are doing so well. Tomorrow Jesus will be burned at the stake by the very people who today have acclaimed him. Jesus listens quietly to the prelate's indignant case against him and the pronouncement of Jesus' being condemned to the fires of the Inquisition. But at the end he stoops to kiss the prelate's cheek in love, and speechless, the old man watches him walk unhindered through the prison door.

Throughout the Gospels, Jesus is the great example of the deliberate rejection of revenge as response to mistreatment. "Do not take revenge on someone who wrongs, you," he says—no matter if someone seeks to exclude you from your own world, and misunderstands and distorts the Kingdom. Jesus lived up to those words in his trial, his appearance before Pilate, his abuse by the soldiers, his crucifixion. "Forgive them, Father, for they do not know what they are doing" (Lk. 23:34). That great freedom from the need to take revenge was evident the first time Jesus came; in his mercy it is still evident in those whom he indwells today.

I long for your merciful help, Lord Jesus, to be as forgiving as you were, as free from hatred and desire for revenge. Amen.

Challenge: Who in your life has been the hardest to forgive, the one against whom the desire for revenge is still lurking? Ask for God's help to give that feeling over into his hands and to let that memory be truly healed.

Mercy Too Late

"You should have had mercy on your fellow servant, just as I had mercy on you" (verse 33).

"When Death, the great Reconciler, has come, it is never our tenderness that we repent of, but our severity."

George Eliot, <u>Adam Bede</u>

Adam, the burly, serious protagonist of George Eliot's novel *Adam Bede,* early in the story looks at the limp drowned corpse of his often drunken father against whom his anger has frequently flared over his coming home intoxicated. The author speaks to us in an aside: "When Death, the great Reconciler, has come, it is never our tenderness that we repent of, but our severity."

Later in the novel, Adam tries to restrain his anger at the man who has seduced his betrothed, Hetty. "There's a sort o' damage, sir, that can't be made up for." Arthur pleads, "Perhaps you've never done anything you've had bitterly to repent of in your life, Adam; if you had, you would be more generous." The waters of memory wash back over Adam's stern nature and he softens. "I was too hard with my father for doing wrong....I've known what it is in my life to repent and feel it's too late....I've no right to be hard toward those as have done wrong and repent."

Anyone who has lived long enough to garner much experience with life can likely write his or her own chapter in that memory book called "Mercy Shown Too Late." Like Adam, who is at times so sternly self-righteous, we plant our feet high on the ladder of our own goodness and prefer to scold rather than comfort the penitent. So often that is the thing he needs least: he already knows his sin. What he needs from us is the encouragement of our admission that we know our own fallibility and can reach out a hand to him and tell him of God's love for sinners. Arthur, without Adam's admission of sorrow over his own stern judgment of his father, would never have become as good a man as he does after Adam confesses his share of common human guilt. We, too, can be a greater help to someone who has stumbled when we recognize that we share with him or her the level ground beneath the cross.

Lord, I long for your saving help to deal with my self-righteousness. May I always recognize the need to love and encourage rather than to condemn. May I have enough of a sense of my own sin that I remember the greatness of mercy. In Jesus' name. Amen.

Challenge: Have you read Dr. Alvin Rogness' book *Forgiveness and Confession: The Keys to Renewal*? If not, why not buy it for your church library—and read it for yourself in the process. (It is available from Augsburg/Fortress.)

The Quality of Mercy

"You are my God, so be merciful to me;..." (verse 3).

"The quality of mercy is not strained,
It droppeth as the gentle rain from heaven
Upon the place beneath. It is twice bless'd;
It blesseth him that gives and him that takes....
Though justice be thy plea, consider this,
That in the course of justice, none of us
Should see salvation: we do pray for mercy;
And that same prayer doth teach us all to render
The deeds of mercy.

William Shakespeare
<u>The Merchant of Venice</u>

How infinitely greater is the mercy of God than that which human beings are likely to show! Using all her young wisdom in an attempt to save her husband's benefactor and friend from Shylock's bond, Portia, in *The Merchant of Venice*, speaks eloquently to the Jewish moneylender about mercy. Her words are so compelling that they have written themselves on many hearts as though they were Scripture. Their hearers are impressed: they nod and all but shout "Amen." Surely Shylock must listen and yield to such pleading. Surely he must realize that his salvation, too, depends not upon justice but upon mercy. And we who read their words, we know that truth for ourselves: it is mercy we need, not justice.

But Shylock will have nothing but his bond. Not mercy. The wily Portia, however, foils his desire for revenge exacted against Antonio. He may have only the pound of flesh, never a drop of blood not granted in the bond. Then it is interesting to see how deep is the belief in mercy among those who have pleaded with Shylock to show mercy. There is no mercy for Shylock. Threatening and taunting, they hound him penniless and daughterless from the house, screaming with laughter at his fear and discomfiture.

Mercy is welcome and dear when we or our side of an issue are in need of it. The need to show it is not half as evident when our opponent or someone unattractive to us puts a claim on our mercy. Shylock, after all, is not very likable.

There is a great deal of insight in Shakespeare's portrayal of this taunting cluster of characters around Shylock. How grateful we should be that the mercy of God is not as fickle and as changeable as our mercy! Surely I will fare badly in any honest judgment unless I have something more rock-like to depend on than my own mercy for others who need it. For in my deserving I am as penniless as Shylock.

God of mercy, thank you that you are not as changeable as we are—as I am. I long for your saving help in being fair in my judgment of others. Amen.

Challenge: Take time to memorize Portia's speech. Keep it in mind to review when you find it hard to be merciful.

Dispossessing Demons

"And you will have authority to drive out demons"
(verse 15).

> *"You know, Manders, the longer I live the more*
> *convinced I am that we're all haunted in this world—*
> *not only by the things we inherit from our parents—*
> *but by the ghosts of innumerable old prejudices and*
> *beliefs—half-forgotten cruelties and betrayals—we*
> *may not even be aware of them—but they're there just*
> *the same—and we can't get rid of them. The whole*
> *world is haunted by these ghosts of the dead past; you*
> *have only to pick up a newspaper to see them weaving*
> *in and out between the lines—Ah! if we only had the*
> *courage to sweep them all out and let in the light!"*
> *Henrik Ibsen, <u>Ghosts</u>*

Henrik Ibsen, the great Norwegian playwright, would likely not have used the term "demons" in the same sense as Mark does, but his plays show a keen concern over those forces which bind human beings and inhibit their abilities to be what they have the potential to be. Jesus, too, knew these evil forces and in his first commissioning of his followers to carry out his healing ministry, he delegated them to use the power he would give them to drive out demons.

In Ibsen's *Ghosts*, Mrs. Alving, speaking intensely to her pastor, a man who seems more concerned with respectability than with healing, expresses her conviction that "we're all haunted in this world—not only by the things we inherit" (as her son has inherited the physical debilities caused by his profligate father's venereal disease) "but by the ghosts of...old prejudices and beliefs—half-forgotten cruelties and betrayals...."

In Ibsen's *Enemy of the People,* the leaders of the town are bound by their love of money even if the gaining of it gives cholera to the tourists who come for the polluted hot mineral baths that attract them to the town. Jesus, with his compassion for those who are possessed and haunted by the many demons that bind them and take away their freedom, promises to work through his followers to drive out demons, to make those who are bound free. "And if the Son sets you free, then you will be really free" (Jn. 8:36). Not many of us call the forces that bind people demons, even though we believe that evil does enter and corrupt lives. But we look daily at a society in which the freedom to live and love and refuse to judge, and to be courageous and to act lovingly for others rather than self is lacking. Individuals are bound in self-centeredness, pettiness, jealousy and hatred. To us in this world where many people are not "O.K.," Jesus promises his power to help set them free to live in the freedom he can give.

Lord, in my relationships with others, I long for your saving help to be the vehicle for your power to set people free from the demons that possess them and distort their lives. Amen.

Challenge: Think of one of your friends that seems haunted and bound by some bitterness or jealousy. Pray that God will use you to set that person free.

Responsibility

"Give strength to hands that are tired and to knees that tremble with weakness" (verse 3).

"The superior man is the providence of the inferior. He is eyes for the blind, strength for the weak, and a shield for the defenseless. He stands erect by bending above the fallen. He rises by lifting others."

Robert G. Ingersoll, "Liberty"

Equality is an attractive concept to some, but a despised one to others. As Americans, we are committed to the concept of equality before the law, though we have a spotty record of providing it. We talk about equality of opportunity, but many sorts of minorities have little access to it. Many kinds of inequalities are built into our physical capabilities and bodies, our social statuses, our economic access to opportunity. Jesus recognized the effects of this in the life of this world. "For the person who has something will be given more, so that he will have more than enough; but the person who has nothing will have taken away from him even the little he has" (Mt. 13:12). The more we know about how our financial system works, the more we know the realism of that statement. The one who has capital to invest is the one who receives the interest.

The Bible reveals a God who loves us all, but its writers are very aware of our differences. They write of the strong and the weak, the good and the evil, the wise and the foolish, the ambitious and the lazy, the rich and the poor, the valiant and the cowardly, the generous and the selfish. Neither physical, spiritual or moral equality are assumed—except the equality of our need of God and his love for us.

The author of our quotation speaks candidly of the superior man and the inferior. These are terms that need to be used carefully because they create a connotation of the innate worth of the individual. It is one thing to admit to the existence of the rich and the poor, the strong and the weak, but another to say that the poor and the weak are inferior in God's sight or our own.

Yet our author and the Biblical writers are in full agreement on the responsibility of the one who demonstrates the characteristics of strength, goodness, wisdom and riches to act as the "providence" of the blind, the weak, the defenseless. "He stands erect by bending above the fallen." Did you notice that? — standing erect by bending? "He rises by lifting others." That is in perfect accord with Isaiah's command to "give strength to hands that are tired and to knees that tremble with weakness." That is what we are here for.

God of compassion, I long for your help to stand erect by bending above those who need strength to arise. Amen.

Challenge: Is there a hospice program in your community? Can you volunteer to give an hour or two to provide some strength for someone who is losing his or hers?

In Deed and In Word

"My children, our love should not be just words and talk; it must be true love, which shows itself in action" (verse 18).

"I like not only to be loved, but also to be told that I am loved. I am not sure that you are of the same kind. But the realm of silence is large enough beyond the grave. This is the world of light and speech, and I shall take leave to tell you that you are very dear."
George Eliot
"Letter to Mrs. Burnes-Jones," May 11, 1875

Have you noticed how often truths are found in what seem to be almost opposite statements—in dichotomies? "That artificial rose is so beautiful it almost looks real," we say, and then are surprised to hear someone else say, "The rose on that bush is so beautiful it almost looks artificial." There is validity in both statements.

We sometimes pose the same kind of paradox in relation to aspects of our Christian faith. "Your actions speak so loudly I cannot hear what you say," says one, only to hear another say in turn, "Let the redeemed of the Lord say so," as someone else says "If you confess with your mouth 'Jesus is Lord,'...you will be saved" (Rom. 10:9).

There is one side of another paradox that says "our love should not be just words and talk; it must be true love, which shows itself in action." But George Eliot provides the "on the other hand" as she writes "I like...to be told that I am loved....and I shall take leave to tell you that you are very dear." As in the instances above, both sides of the paradox have something to tell us.

Most of us find few things so repulsive as the sentimental gush of insincere avowals of affection. I quit going to a dress shop I really liked because of a syrupy clerk who always addressed me as "Honey." But many of us offend more seriously by our reluctance to speak our love to those who need to hear that they are loved. It would be interesting to know how many of our acquaintances we know have never heard anyone say to them "I love you." I think we would be shocked to know how large the number would be. Many of those people would be shocked into shyness if before the day is done we broke out of our inhibitions and said, "You know, I really love you." How difficult that kind of loving openness is to us!

Yet how empty those words would be if they were not accompanied by acts that reinforce them. We would not long believe those words. But why can we not give both the words and the actions? We don't need to worry about running out of the supply of love. "You yourselves have been taught by God how you should love one another," Paul writes to the Thessalonian believers. "Do even more." Have we already been loving in word and deed? There is Paul's daily assignment for us in the school of life: DO EVEN MORE.

Lord of love and compassion, I long for your Spirit's help to make me a vessel through which your love can flow freely to others, both in word and in deed. May I do even more. Amen.

Challenge: Who among your daily associates is the hardest to really love in word and deed? Really pray for them for the coming two weeks, and watch what happens to your feelings for them.

Sweet Singers

"But if we hope for what we do not see, we wait for it with patience" (verse 25).

"Hope is the thing with feathers
That perches in the soul,
And sings the tune without the words,
And never stops at all."

Emily Dickinson
"Hope Is the Thing with Feathers"

What an excellent analogy exists between hope and a bird—"the thing with feathers That perches in the soul." Hope is such a tenuous thing, and a bird is—or most birds are—such precarious little beings. One has no sooner said such a thing, however, than one remembers the distance traveled by those little wings that carry the hummingbirds from Canada to South America. And the surprising durability of hope.

Have you ever watched a bird trying to perch on a telephone wire in a strong wind? Marvelously designed as they are, the feet can hardly hold their grip on the wire, and if the bird had not been wise enough to perch facing the wind it would have been ruffled and tattered and turned quite inside out. Hope, too, perches in the soul facing adversity, facing grief or emptiness or tumult, but holding tight to the promises God has given us.

How often in our deepest trouble we, like the bird, sing without being able to find the words. The words belong to faith and truth; hope is still reaching out for them. The sounds may be beautiful but their thoughts are yet to be articulated. But the song goes on and on; it "never stops at all." That is the nature of hope—to hold on.

Have you ever listened for the birds in a blizzard or a bitter storm wind? They seem to have left; they cannot be seen. But let a lull come or the wind abate, there is the chickadee at your feeder. Chipping and chirping, its song is as sweet as ever. It cannot be long abashed if it is to survive in such weather!

To look at the other side of our analogy, have you noticed how hope survives in the storms of life almost better than in its calms? The calms make few demands on hope; hope can lose its muscle tone from lack of exercise. The bird who sat on its nest all summer would be a poor candidate for successful migration.

Life would be dreary indeed if it were not for the "thing with feathers That perches in the soul." One wonders if it isn't the absence of it that takes the expression out of many people's faces. Hopelessness is often the curse of our inner cities and rural slums, with their unemployment and poverty. Abraham, Paul reminds us (Rom. 4:18), "hoped, even when there was no reason for hoping," and became the father of a nation. So, too, we can hold fast. "Let your hope keep you joyful, be patient in your troubles, and pray at all times" (Rom. 12:12).

I long for your saving hope, O Lord, to keep my hopes built on nothing less than your blood and righteousness, knowing that "in every high and stormy gale" you will continue to be my hope and stay. Amen.

Challenge: Think about what could be the worst possible thing that could happen to you. Right now put that thing into God's hands and from this moment concentrate on letting your hope keep you joyful.

A Perpetual Court

*"When, Lord, did we ever see you hungry or thirsty,
or a stranger or naked or sick or in prison, and we
would not help you?" (verse 44).*

*"Only our concept of Time makes it possible for
us to speak of the Day of Judgment by that name; in
reality it is a summary court in perpetual session."*
        Frank Kafka, <u>Letters</u> (quoted by Max Brod)

Frank Kafka's writings are often obscure because
of his unusual use of symbols, but in his novel *The Trial*
he sets in motion a character with which every individual has some similarities, and with whom many in
our day have felt sympathy. This man awakens one
morning in his rooming house, expecting to go to work
as usual. Instead he finds himself apprehended by men
who seem to be law officers, who tell him he is to be
brought to trial. They are very unclear about the nature
of the charges, about the time of the trial, about what he
can do to defend himself or clear his name. Nothing the
accused can do, whether going to the court or trying to
change lawyers, can clarify his status or the punish-
ment that awaits him. At the end he is no more certain
of what he has done wrong than at the beginning. Some
critics have called him the perfect representation of the
spiritual state of modern man. He is at the mercy of a
"summary court in perpetual session," with a sense of
malaise, but unable to be sure what is wrong.

When Jesus talks about judgment he is far more
specific about what it is based on and what constitutes
guilt. When he is asked to identify the essence of the
law, he says it consists of the love of God with heart,
soul, and mind—and one's neighbor as oneself (Mt.

22:37-39). And how does that love that satisfies the law reveal itself? In giving what is needed to others: food, drink, shelter, clothes, care and acceptance.

We live out this ministry called for by law and fulfilled by love, not in a few great appearances before the court of God at which verdict is rendered. In a real sense, we, too, face a court in perpetual session. We face a law that evaluates act and attitude throughout our lives.

We find greater comfort in Paul's "We know that a person is put right with God only through faith in Jesus Christ, never by what the law requires" (Gal. 2:16). Yet we know, too, that, accepting our justification through faith, we still must take seriously the words of Jesus. He says that from us who have been given the gifts (Mt. 25:31-40) will be expected the kind of love that shows itself in a constant sharing of what we have with others. That obligation is not over at the end of the fiscal year. The memory bank of God's computer works more accurately than does Kafka's trial court.

I long for your saving grace, O Lord, to help me see in every human being one to whom I have the on-going obligation of love and assistance. Amen.

Challenge: Think through how you have handled your responsibility to minister to someone in prison. What specific thing can you do?

A New Kind of Trap

"Get out of the trap like a bird or deer escaping from a hunter" (verse 5).

"But why are these men always tired? Is it the jobs they hold, the kind of men who stop in at this tavern? Why do they flash their teeth when they smile, but stop smiling so quickly? Why do their children cringe from them sometimes—...? Why do they grow old so quickly, sitting at kitchen tables with bottles of beer? They are everywhere, in every house..."

Joyce Carol Oates, "Four Summers"

In Joyce Oates' "Four Summers," we see the central character in the same setting, a lakeside bar-restaurant, during four significant summers. First she is a small, pretty child, hanging on her mother's skirts as the parents drink a succession of beers and carry on inane conversations with friends of their own type. In the second scene, she and her brother plague the already soused father to take them for a boat ride, at the end of which he vomits drunkenly over the side of the boat. In the scene from the third summer, she flirts with a man in the parking lot as her parents drink inside, but runs from him, frightened by his kiss. By the fourth summer she is married and pregnant, trying to avoid the realization that her husband is a repeat version of her father as she is of her mother. She sits at the bar wondering why the men she has seen at home and at the bar look so bored with life.

To the girl it seems as if their lives are "like cards dealt out to them in their innumerable card games." In her succinctly created scenes, Oates has presented characters whose building materials for their lives have no more substance than the plasticized cards. One beer after another, one gossip session after another, hours of unproductive apathy in the face of boredom, they can build of their lives only shanties rather than homes for the children they bring into the world. Ironically, that kind of life is the only one their children know, and all too often they play a repeat performance.

How tragic that they let life happen to them rather than take hold of life and build of it a structure that can stand in the face of boredom and frustration! How sad the children, who in the growing up see and hear nothing but carping and cantankerousness about them! God doesn't intend for us to be unresisting victims, doomed to repeat the emptiness of generations before us.

But who is to step in to put some solid footing under the lives of children so afflicted? Does the fact that *we* live next door or down the street offer us the opportunity to let those children see a different kind of life—a life that is deliberately shaped into something meaningful, life that reaches out to bored and unloved children, a life that has promise for the future?

Lord, I feel pity for those whose lives seem nothing but boredom and emptiness. I long for your power and love to be of help as you have been to me. Amen.

Challenge: Is there a family or a child in your neighborhood that needs you to become involved in helping them see a higher way?

The Danger of Familiarity

*"For when we loved according to our human nature,
the sinful desires stirred up by the Law were at work
in our bodies and we were useful in the service of
death" (verse 5).*

*"Vice is a monster of so frightful mien,
As to be hated needs but to be seen;
Yet seen too oft, familiar with her face,
We first endure, then pity, then embrace.*
Alexander Pope, Essay on Man

Let us see often enough someone who at first strikes
us as ugly, and we will soon find his looks more acceptable than at first. Let us hear often enough a shocking
idea, and before long we have accommodated ourselves to it. Let us accustom ourselves to doing what
has previously been objectionable, and before long we
do it without even being aware. Is it not so?

I find it amazing how many customs or practices
that were frowned upon in my childhood and in my
home town are now entirely acceptable, not only there
but almost everywhere. We have become used to such
rapid changes on the national and international scene.
One day China is our enemy. We are convinced of that!
But let our national leaders decide almost overnight
that it is in our national interest that China be our
friend, and see how fast the rhetoric can change. No
wonder, when change can come so rapidly on such
major issues, the old warnings against tawdry movies,
dancing, drinking, smoking, immodest dress, and gambling can fade so quickly.

Much undesirable legalism faded deservedly along
with those warnings. A picture is not wrong because it

moves; rhythmic movement can be a natural pleasure; gambling may not always create an appetite for higher stakes; smoking is better fought on arguments of health than of morality.

Yet doesn't Pope express a principle of human response in which we may find truth when he reminds us that continued exposure to vice, to what is morally dubious, does work a change in our attitudes? Not knowing how to fight it successfully, we do nothing— we endure. Finding ourselves sympathetic to the one or the act being criticized, we pity. Finding advantages in what has previously been rejected, we do not want to be left out and we embrace the very thing we have first assessed as having a "frightful mien."

"To be useful in the service of death" is not our aim as Christians. Legalism may enlist us in that service as surely as license (uncontrolled behavior). Christian freedom may, by our desire to please the Father, lead us to reject the same practices that legalism scolds against, but the motivation is different. Looking through the eyes of faith and love, we may serve life by turning our backs on the "monster" which God hates.

Lord of holiness and purity, I long for your Spirit's help that I may look through your eyes at vice and sin and have the same opinion of them that you do. Amen.

Challenge: Examine your life carefully to see if some vice is hidden and protected because of unwillingness to recognize how your attitude toward it has grown more tolerant.

In the Stillness

"After the earthquake there was a fire—but the Lord was not in the fire. And after the fire there was the soft whisper of a voice" (verse 12).

"In the ordinary course of nature, the great beneficient changes come slowly and silently. The noisy changes, for the most part, mean violence and disruption. The roar of storms and tornadoes, the explosion of volcanoes, the crash of the thunder, are the result of a sudden break in the equipoise of the elements; from a condition of comparative repose and silence they become fearfully swift and audible. The still small voice is the voice of life and growth and perpetuity....In the history of a nation it is the same.

John Burroughs
"An Outlook on Life," Leaf and Tendril

At different times in the history of God's people he deals with them in varying ways. The prophets record these methods in their writings. Isaiah, for example, speaks of the deliverance that God will bring his people. "Suddenly and unexpectedly the Lord Almighty will rescue you with violent thunderstorms and earthquakes. He will send windstorms and raging fire;..." (29:6). In contrast, when God speaks to the despondent Elijah, who is sure that he is the only remaining believer, we are specifically told that the Lord was *not* in the "furious wind that split the hills," *not* in the earthquake, *not* in the fire, but in the "soft whisper of a voice." It is the whisper that gives Elijah the command that will enable him to be God's prophet to Ahab and Jezebel and their Baal-worshipping followers.

Sometimes people are convinced by the loud and catastrophic events, and remember how God has acted through them. Often those events seem to be easy to forget, and people go back to their old ways with amazing ease. As Burroughs, that keen observer, believes that "the great beneficient changes come slowly and silently," so we, too, may observe that not only in nature but in the history of a nation and the lives of individuals "the still small voice is the voice of life and growth and perpetuity."

Elijah responded to the still small voice. The prophets who thundered against the sins of the people had their individual calls to be God's messengers in private conversations with him—no need to shout. Gabriel comes to the Virgin Mary in a quiet encounter. Jesus first reveals who he is in a well-side conversation with the Samaritan woman. When Jesus arrests Paul on the road to Damascus, only Paul hears the words that Jesus speaks. As we think of what we know of God's dealings with human beings down through the ages, the quiet single encounters are most often what sets off the conversions, the commissionings, and the miracles.

Surely God is speaking in the traumatic and dramatic events of life, and we need to listen for their interpretations spoken to our hearts by the Spirit of God. But, even more likely it is in our noise-wracked world that God speaks to us in the quiet of his Word, in our prayer times, in the silence of each time we are willing to listen.

Lord, keep me so alert to your still small voice that I do not need the discipline of the "fearfully swift and audible." Amen.

Challenge: Take some minutes to ponder Burroughs' theory that "the great beneficient changes come slowly and silently. The noisy changes, for the most part, mean violence and disruption." What evidence can you find that what he suggests is true?

The Greatest Message

"Then the other disciple, who had reached the tomb first, also went in; he saw and believed" (verse 8).

"Jesus was the only One that ever raised the dead," the Misfit continued, "and He shouldn't have done it. He's thrown everything off balance. If he did what He said, then it's nothing for you to do but throw away everything and follow Him, and if He didn't, then it's nothing for you to do but enjoy the few minutes you got left the best way you can...."

Flannery O'Connor
"A Good Man Is Hard to Find"

Many truths are combined in the story that brings us the Gospel message; to try to arrange them in order of importance is as fruitless as trying to decide whether Easter or Christmas is the more important Christian holy-day. The book of Acts is full of emphasis on the resurrection. Both Peter and Paul proclaim it as the center of their message. As we read Acts we see its effect on the frightened believers; they become infused with a power beyond their own. They "saw and believed."

The "Misfit" of Flannery O'Connor's story had almost as keen an insight into the significance of Jesus' power over death as did the preachers of the book of Acts. All of his life an outcast, he is a criminal who has just shot one victim to death and is holding a gun on a trembling grandmother who tries to appeal to his "better" self. He nevertheless realizes, with more profundity than most of those who have heard the Jesus story, what Jesus' resurrection involves. "If He did what he said, then it's nothing for you to do but to throw away everything and follow him, and if he didn't, then it's nothing for you to do but enjoy the few minutes you got left the best way you can...." The style may not be that of the theologian, but what is said makes good theology.

The demand of the Jesus story is to be taken seriously. The story of a dying god is present in many of the world's religions. The story of One who has power over death and rose to change the course of human history is unique. Either we recognize the power and uniqueness of that story, or else, as the Misfit recognizes, the "few minutes" of this life are all there will be. The Misfit doesn't question that Jesus raised the dead. But he is not willing to surrender to the call to "throw away everything and follow him." Therefore, he will kill as he is threatening to do, because the alternative is to "enjoy the few minutes you got left."

I wonder if the powerful demands of the Gospel on those who hear it is not often deadened for us by the fact that we have heard it so often; we are so religiously sophisticated. O'Connor's killer has heard that story and recognized its implication. There is no being the same after one has heard that story. Willingly, or even unwittingly, one has made a decision about its significance.

God of life and power and resurrection, I long for your help to understand the implications for my life of the power Jesus revealed over death. Amen.

Challenge: Look very thoroughly at the alternatives the Misfit set up. Have you dealt with them for yourself?

Excelsior

"Let us go forward then, to mature teaching...." (verse 2).

> *"Why build these cities glorious*
>   *If man [a human being] unbuilded goes?*
>   Edwin Markham, "Man-Making"*

One can hear a note of impatience behind the writer's words as he tells these Hebrew Christians how difficult it is to explain spiritual truths to them because they are so slow to understand. If they had responded to his teaching as he had expected, they should have been teachers by now, not still busy with their spiritual ABCs. Paul had had the same experience with the Corinthian Christians—"I had to feed you milk, not solid food, because you were not ready for it" (I Cor. 3:2).

Parents are soon alarmed, as are doctors, by a growing child's inability to take solid food. Teachers find it easy to sympathize with Paul and the author of Hebrews because they are so often frustrated by what seems to be total indifference on the part of some students to basic skills needed for further learning.

Analysts ponder what keeps the church from the kind of effectiveness it might have. Is it lack of leadership? lack of money? lack of facilities? Is it not rather, in part at least, that too few in the church have any deep concern about spiritual growth? that so many who have lived all their lives in the church are almost totally inarticulate about their faith? that they have little ability to apply what they have heard in hundreds of sermons to distinguish between good and evil—or little desire to? Many congregations operate at starvation level as far as their adult education programs go.

Our pastors must often agree with Paul when he writes, "I could not talk to you as I talk to people who have the Spirit; I had to talk to you as though you belonged to this world, as children in the Christian faith" (I Cor. 3:1). Which are we—the adult Christians who know their need of spiritual growth, or the "babes of Christ" who "still need someone to teach [us] the first lessons"? "Let us go forward!" pleads the author of Hebrews.

We find food in the bread and wine of the communion table. We need to find the divine Word opened to us in the Sunday sermon. But we also need to come to that Word in individual study, with the Holy Spirit as our teacher, and to study it with other believers, sharing our insights with each other.

"There has been time enough for you to be teachers." Is that what we are?

O Lord, I long for your Spirit's help that I may hunger and thirst for the Bread of Life and the Water of Life freely given me in your Word. May I not be an example of spiritual malnourishment. Amen.

Challenge: What is your individual plan for spiritual growth? What part of it is directed at "solid food" beyond "milk"? Re-evaluate your plan in terms of what will make you ready to be a teacher.

A Treasured Gift

"...for so he giveth his beloved sleep" (verse 2).

"Of all the thoughts of God that are
Borne inward into souls afar,
Along the Psalmist's music deep,
Now tell me if that any is,
For gift or grace, surpassing this:
He giveth his beloved—sleep."
E. B. Browning, "The Sleep"

Researchers in our day are studying sleep—what happens when we sleep, how much sleep we need, what effect the loss of it has on us, and more. We differ in the amount of sleep we need and the time we spend in dreams. But we all need sleep; we all suffer if we lack it. Most of us complain if we find it hard to achieve. We even pray for it:

O may my soul in thee repose,
And may sweet sleep mine eyelids close,
Sleep that shall me more vigorous make
To serve my God when I awake.

(LBW 278, verse 4)

Elizabeth Barrett Browning was for much of her life an invalid. She must often have felt that days were long, and without normal physical activity sleep was hard to achieve. No wonder in her situation she came to look upon sleep as a gift of grace—"He giveth his beloved sleep."

Sleep in Scripture is used in many contexts. The psalmists frequently use it in the same sense Browning does. Other writers look at it as an evidence of lethargy and laziness. Some poets use it as a type of death, the one who "falls asleep" as one who "wraps the drapery of his couch about him and lies down to pleasant dreams" (W. C. Bryant). Donne calls sleep a "shadow" of death ("Death, Be Not Proud"). Since most of us spend over a fourth of our lives in sleep, it is not strange that we pay it so much attention.

Many people have believed that God communicates with us in our sleep by dreams. We are frequently told in Scripture of God speaking to people while they slept—Jacob, Samuel, Joseph (husband of Mary). Perhaps few of us experience such direct communication with God in our sleep or dreams, but certainly the time when we are wakeful in the night is a time for us both to speak to God and to listen for God to speak to us. The One who gives us sleep is near and listening.

I have long remembered, in a session led by a saintly elderly speaker, a woman told how often, when she got to bed and composed her thoughts to pray, she found herself drifting off to sleep before the prayer was more than begun, and then felt so guilty. The eyes of the speaker twinkled, and he replied so gently, "What a wonderful way to go to sleep!" What precious comfort—for "he giveth his beloved sleep."

I long for your comfort, O Lord, for those who because they grieve or feel stress or struggle with some trouble or illness find it hard to sleep. In their wakefulness may their conversation with you be precious to them. Amen.

Challenge: Think through your personal sleep patterns. Is there a time during your nights for some moments of meditation? Read a book on Christian meditation and learn how to put it to use in your life.

All in Order

*"Throughout our lives we are always in danger of
death for Jesus' sake" (verse 11).*

> *"Whenever I prepare for a journey I prepare as
> though for death. Should I never return, all is in
> order. This is what life has taught me."*
> Kathryn Mansfield, *Journal* (1922)

I recognized a kindred spirit in Kathryn Mansfield
in her attitude toward practical preparation for death.
For years I have tried never to leave unpaid bills when I
leave town. If something should happen to me while I
am gone from home, my creditor will have his money
far more easily than if he has to wait for probate or
convenience from someone else. I do not find that concern morbid; I find it practical. It eases my mind. For in
spite of all we have learned about prolonging life, as
futurist Ted Peters reminds us, "the death rate is still
100%."

It is strange that we who have the glorious hope of
life beyond death are so often fearful of death or the
speaking about it. We have heard the story of the slave
who upon his master's death was asked if he believed
his master had gone to heaven. "No, suh, he allus tol' us
when he was goin' to Atlanta or to Nashville, but he
never said nothin' 'bout goin' to heaven." Are we equally
reticent?

Paul had a beautiful freedom of talking about death
and union with his Lord. As he listened to the eleven
speak of the experiences they had had in their intimate
walk with Jesus, he must have longed for an experience
like theirs. One day he, too, would sit and talk with the
One who had arrested him that day on the Damascus

road. "For what is life?" he wrote to the Philippian believers. "To me, it is Christ. Death then will bring more....I am pulled in two directions. I want very much to leave this life and be with Christ, which is a far better thing;..." (Phil. 1:21, 23).

We feel good to know as we leave home in the morning that "should I never return, all is in order," as Mansfield says. Even more important it is to know that spiritually all is in order, that our lives are committed to God, our loved ones through prayer are placed confidently in God's keeping, and if accident or illness stills our heartbeat or brain waves, all is well.

Lord, when the tempest rages, I need not fear;
For you, the Rock of Ages, Are always near.
Close by your side abiding I fear no foe,
For when your hand is guiding In peace I go.
Lord, when the shadows lengthen And night has come,
I know that you will strengthen My steps toward home,
And nothing can impede me, O blessed Friend!
So take my hand and lead me Unto the end.

(LBW, 233)

Challenge: If you have not yet made your will, take a first step toward doing so. If there is someone who should know the location of that document, tell them.

The Mortal Exception

"When you plant a seed in the ground, it does not sprout to life unless it dies" (verse 36).

"Ivan Ilych saw that he was dying, and he was in continual despair…not only was he not accustomed to the thought, he simply did not and could not grasp it.

The syllogism he had learnt from Kiezewetter's Logic: 'Caius is a man, men are mortal, therefore Caius is mortal,' had always seemed to him correct as applied to Caius, but certainly not as applied to himself."

Leo Tolstoy, <u>The Death of Ivan Ilych</u>

Long before modern psychologists had outlined for us the stages a dying person is likely to pass through, the great Russian novelist Tolstoy created a powerfully realistic portrayal of a man going from health through agonizing illness to the experience of death. The insight is penetrating: we watch his family move from fear and sympathy to a resentment at having their lives constricted by his prolonged illness. His own pain is increased by his sensing that no one, not even his doctor, is being honest with him about his condition. And when his friends receive news of his death, "the first thought of each of the gentlemen…was of the changes and promotions it might occasion among themselves or their acquaintances." At the funeral, they plan in whispers the evening card party.

As Ivan faces the reality of his approaching death, he resists acceptance of the inevitability of death as it applies to him. Mortality?—that is all right for Caius in the schoolboy syllogism. But must he accept it for himself? Indeed, he finds no alternative. Slowly and painfully he "struggled in that black sack into which he was being thrust by an invisible, resistless force." But just as he feels the kiss of his young son, sees the undried tears on his wife's face, and feels sympathy for them, and just as he recalls that what has been wrong in his life can be rectified by grace, he catches sight of a light at the bottom of the black sack, and the pain is gone. When someone near him hears the death rattle and says "It is finished," he can within himself say "Death is finished." The cynicism and despair of the starkly realistic story has changed to the calm and resignation of a peaceful death. The "seed" of Ivan Ilych has been planted in the ground and in its time will sprout into new life.

St. Paul knows the importance of the faith in a resurrection life in the early church. Some members had doubted, and so he writes his magnificent treatise on the essential nature of that belief. There is no denial of the reality of death. Even Paul's Resurrection Lord has tasted that experience and the pain that led to it. But another chapter comes. What is buried is "ugly and weak" like the wracked body of Ivan Ilych, but "when raised, it will be beautiful and strong."

Thank you, O Christ, for sharing even the experiences of pain and death with us in order that we may share the experience of glory and eternal health with you. Amen.

Challenge: Do you know someone in Ivan's condition of approaching death? Take a half hour to spend with him or her in loving support.

Patriotism or Chauvinism

*"You are going to hear the noise of battles close by
and the news of battles far away;..." (verse 6).*

*"In the days to come, as through all time that is
past, man will lord it over his fellow, and earth will be
stained red from veins of young and old. That sweet
and sounding name of **patria** becomes an illusion and
a curse."*

George Gissing, <u>By the Ionian Sea</u>

To many people, the word *patriotism* is uncondi-
tionally a good word, seldom if ever, to be questioned.
To them Gissing's statement that the "sweet and sounding name of *patria*" can become "an illusion and a
curse" would be radical and unthinkable. Gissing, as-
sessing the past, predicts that man will ever "lord it
over his fellow, and earth will be stained red from veins
of young and old" because of a false patriotism that
puts allegiance to a country or a government ahead of
respect for life and the well-being of other humans.

In one sense, patriotism is a good and inspiring
thing. It recognizes and respects all that humans have
done to govern themselves wisely and well. It is related
to the productivity and beauty of the land. It helps to
give a feeling of identity and rootedness. Loyalty to
one's country is linked to one's history and one's family, and encourages a sense of belonging and unity in a
community.

But terrible things have been done in the name of
patriotism. Persecutions and pogroms, massacres and
wars have been bred by chauvinistic patriotism. People
have been belittled, both individually and as groups.
They have been deprived and made refugees by the

false belief that national boundaries determine human worth. History is replete with accounts of those who use national identity and pride in it to oppress and plunder.

Jesus, knowing human nature as he did, knew that there was little likelihood that war would ever be far from humanity—"You are going to hear the noise of battles close by and...far away." But it is our duty as human beings and as Christians not to use love and loyalty for our country to count ourselves as of more worth than others, or favor policies that plunder their resources for our enrichment, or suppose that God loves us more than others. There are already too many of these behaviors recorded in the human story.

> From war's alarms, from deadly pestilence,
> Make your strong arm our ever sure defense.
> Your true religion in our hearts increase;
> Your boundless goodness nourish us in peace.
> Amen.
> (LBW, 567)

God of all time and nations, give us a love for your creation and all people that will help us to rise above chauvinism and artificial boundaries. Keep us from supposing that you show favoritism to the rich and the oppressor. Amen.

Challenge: Determine to evaluate our behavior as a nation as realistic as we do that of other nations. Use your right of free speech to insist that we act morally as a nation.

After Christmas

"The Word became a human being and, full of grace and truth, lived among us" (verse 14).

"Well, so that is that. Now we must dismantle the tree,
Putting the decorations back into their cardboard boxes—..."

W. H. Auden, "After Christmas"

If our finite minds could ever really get hold of the implications of that Scripture verse, "The Word became a human being and...lived among us," Christmas as we experience it would have a different kind of spiritual impact. Could we ever say on the day after it, "Well, so that is that," and go on to dismantle the tree, already turning our minds from the words "For unto you is born this day a Savior." "The Word became a human being...and lived among us"?

For a month ahead of time the carols have rung from the department store loudspeakers; the Advent candles have been lighted in churches and in Christian homes; children have memorized their "pieces" and looked in awe at the huge trees in the chancels. Gifts for purchase and for wrapping have piled the counters high since before Thanksgiving, but decreasing numbers of even church members have thought it important to go to God's house at Thanksgiving. After all, it is almost Christmas.

Then comes Christmas Eve and the special Day, and those who have come home for Christmas leave again, and the lovely wrappings now in shreds are hustled off to the refuse container. Meals become leftovers, and the parents collapse in the only chairs not piled high with gifts, and let-down sets in. A let-down? "The Word became a human being...and lived among us." How can there be a let-down after that? What has gone wrong?

The tense of the verb. That is what has gone wrong. So long as the tense is past tense—he lived among us—then Christmas, however lovely, can quickly slip into the past. But when we come to appreciate that tense is no limitation on God, that "he lived among us" is truly "he lives among us," then we can know that Christmas is an eternal present. Its joy and power are always available to us. It is not, as Auden says, "Well, so that is that" just for the time being; it is forever.

That doesn't mean we have to survive for the whole year the hubbub we endure for most of December. That could get any of us down. But it need not be true for us that once again we have failed to catch the significance of the vision or to believe in its reality.

We long for your saving help, O Lord, that the great spiritual moments of our lives may empower us not only "for the time being" but forever, in the troughs of life as well as on its peaks. Amen.

Challenge: Think through your personal Christmas traditions and celebrations. How could they be changed or rearranged to increase their spiritual impact through more of the year?

Translation

"The Lord buried him in a valley in Moab...but to this day no one knows the exact place of his burial" (verse 6).

"And when she [the church] buries a man, that action concerns me: all mankind is of one author, and is one volume; when one man dies, one chapter is not torn out of the book, but translated into a better language; and every chapter must be so translated; God employs several translators; some pieces are translated by age, some by sickness, some by war, some by justice; but God's hand is in every translation, and his hand shall bind up all our scattered leaves again for that library where every book shall lie open to one another."

John Donne, "Meditation XVII"

All of Moses' life, except when he lived with the family of Jethro in the wilderness, was a very public life. His childhood and young manhood were spent in a palace; the last forty years, except for the time on Mt. Sinai, was constantly lived out among his people. But how different his death! The most total privacy any of us can know—just God and Moses. I often wondered about the reason for that hidden burial place until a modern rabbi suggested to me that if Moses' grave had been known it would have become a place of idolatry. His descendants would have made pilgrimages to pay homage, as Moslems do to Mecca. The hidden grave kept the attention on Moses' God, not on the man himself, as Torah demanded.

John Donne, seventeenth century clergyman and poet, looked upon the burial of a believer in a different way. To him a man's life is a volume of many pages— each day a page?—in one language and by one author. When the cover is closed and that book complete, it is time for it to be translated into another language—a better one. Some are translated by age to this finer language, some by war, some by illness. The Owner of the library is active in the process—indeed, he is said to observe even the death of the sparrow. When the process is complete, the book is not hidden secretly in the library as Moses was in Moab, an enemy land. Instead each book is tidied and laid open for others to read. Its blessings for others are not done yet. Each book tells the story of how the Owner has brought it into being. It illuminates other lives whose stories are still to be translated. Seldom will the translation bring about false worship or idolatrous veneration. Rather, each new translation will be an encouragement to those who come after. All who enter that library are aware that each new translation is a matter of the Owner's grace and artistry, not of their labors. Heaven can be envisioned as the joyful revealing of the stories told by those open pages and the glorification of the Owner.

Great Owner of my life, I long for your help to ensure that the translation of my messy copybook into your great Book of Life may be all to your glory. Amen.

Challenge: If you have not already done so, write in a notebook the story of your life, telling especially how the Owner is making you ready for translation.

List of Sources

1. The Collected Poems of G. K. Chesterton. New York: Dodd, Mead and Company, 1932.
5. New York: Harper and Brothers Publishers, 1927.
7. George B. Hill edition, Vol. I. New York: Octagon Books, 1967.
9. The Journal of George Fox. London: J. M. Dent and Sons, Ltd., 1924.
11. The Complete Poems and Plays, 1909-1950. New York: Harcourt, Brace, and World, Inc., 1952.
13. The Norton Anthology of Modern Poetry, Richard Ellman and Robert O'Clair, eds. New York: W. W. Norton Company, Inc., 1973.
15. The Complete Works of Montaigne, Donald M. Frame, trans. Stanford, CA: Stanford University Press, 1948.
17. The Complete Poems of Robert Frost. New York: Holt, Rinehart, and Winston, 1949.
19. Hawthorne's Short Stories. New York: Alfred A. Knopf, 1969.
21. New York: Ballantine Books, 1965.
23. The Collected Poems of W. B. Yeats. New York: Macmillan Company, 1956.
25. New York: Harpers Magazine Press, 1974.
27. New York: Random House, 1946.
29. Katherine Woods, trans. New York: Harcourt, Brace and World, 1943.
31. Humphrey Carpenter, ed. Boston: Houghton Mifflin Company, 1981.
33. Boston: Houghton Mifflin Company, 1933.
35. The Poems and Fairy Tales of Oscar Wilde. New York: Modern Library, 1932.
37. New York: Charles Scribner's Sons, 1927.
39. David Magarshack, trans. Baltimore: Penguin Books, 1958.
41. The History of Tom Jones, a Foundling. New York: The Heritage Press, 1952.
43. Poems and Essays. New York: Vintage Books, 1924.
45. The Complete Stories of Flannery O'Connor. New York: Farrar, Strauss, and Giroux, 1971.

47. The Triumph of an Egg. New York: B. W. Huebeck, Inc., MCMXXI.

49. New and Collected Poems, 1917-1976. Boston: Houghton Mifflin Company, 1976.

51. Collected Poems. Garden City, New York: Doubleday, 1961.

53. Robert Frost, op. cit.

55. Walden and Other Writings, Joseph Krutch, ed. Bantam Classic. New York: Bantam Books, 1962.

57. Edwin Way Teale, ed. Boston: Houghton Mifflin Company, 1954.

59. The Complete Poetical Works of Wordsworth. Boston: Houghton Mifflin Company, 1932.

61. In the Heart of the Heart of the Country and Other Stories. New York: Harper and Row, Publishers, 1968.

63. Francis Thompson, Poems and Essays, Wilfred Meynell, ed. Freeport, New York: Books for Libraries Press, 1947.

65. Boston: Houghton Mifflin Company, 1966.

67. Byron, Lord. Leslie Marchand, ed. Boston: Riverside Press, 1935.

69. The Complete Poems of Carl Sandburg. New York: Harcourt, Brace and World, Inc., 1950.

71. T. S. Eliot, op. cit.

73. The Collected Stories of Isaac Bashevis Singer. New York: Farrar, Strauss and Giroux, 1982.

75. The Complete Works of Shakespeare, G. L. Kittredge, ed. Boston: Ginn and Company, 1936. (III,iii).

77. New York: Dell Publishing Company, 1973.

79. Life and Speeches of William Jennings Bryan. New York: The Abbey Press, 1902-1907.

81. The Complete Poetry and Selected Prose of John Donne. New York: The Modern Library, 1941.

83. Poems, 1940-1953. New York: Random House, 1953.

85. New York: Bantam Books, 1946.

87. Poems of Arthur Hugh Clough. London: Macmillan and Company, 1888.

89. The Poetical Works of Alfred, Lord Tennyson. New York: Thomas Y. Crowell and Company, 1885.

91. The Poetical Works of William Cullen Bryant (Roslyn Edition). New York: AMS Press, 1969.

93. T. S. Eliot, op. cit.

95. Shakespeare, op. cit. (V, v).

97. The Complete Short Stories of Robert Louis Stevenson, Charles Neider, ed. Garden City, N. Y.: Doubleday, 1969.

99. Vol. I (1760), 12. London: George Rutledge and Sons. n.d.

101. Poems of Gerard Manley Hopkins, Robert Bridges, ed. London: Oxford University Press, 1930.

103. In The New Masses, December, 1926.

105. Discourses as Reported by Arrian, W. A. Oldfather (Vol. I, Book II, xviii). Cambridge, MA: Harvard University Press, 1961.

107. R. T. Lowe-Porter, trans. New York: Alfred A. Knopf, 1965.

109. Stuart Gilbert, trans. New York: The Modern Library, 1948.

111. Source unknown.

113. The Collected Poetry of Robinson Jeffers, Tim Hunt, ed. (Vol. I, 1920-1928). Stanford, CA: Stanford University Press, 1988.

115. Mr. Dooley at His Best, Elmer Ellis, ed. New York: Charles Scribner's Sons, 1938.

117. The Satires of Juvenal, Ralph Humphries, trans. "On Education in Avarice." Bloomington, IN: Indiana University Press, 1958.

119. History of the Plague Years in London, 1665, to which is added...the essay in verse "The True-Born Englishman, a Satire." London: G. Bell and Sons, 1908.

121. The Complete Short Stories of D. H. Lawrence in Three Volumes (III). London: William Heineman, 1955.

123. Six Plays by Henrik Ibsen, Eva Le Gallienne, trans. New York: Modern Library, 1951.

125. The Autobiography of Benjamin Franklin and Selections from His Writings. New York: Random House, 1944.

127. New York: Ballantine Books, 1965. (The Fellowship of the Ring).

129. Freeport, New Jersey: Book of Libraries Press, 1971.

131. Steps to the Temple. The Poems of Richard Crashaw. London: Random House, 1957.

133. The Plays of Eugene O'Neill (Scene I). New York: Random House, 1920.

135. Francis Thompson, op. cit.

137. New York: Ballantine Books, 1965. (The Return of the King).

139. "Essays on Faith and Morals." New York: World Publishing Company, 1897.

141. New York: Charles Scribner's Sons, 1948.

143. Collected Verse of Rudyard Kipling. Garden City, N.Y.: Doubleday Page and Company, 1922.

145. New York: Oxford University Press, 1953.

147. The Women Poets in English, Ann Stanford, ed. New York: McGraw Hill Company, 1972.

149. Alan Paton, op. cit.

151. New York: Modern Library College Editions, 1952.

153. New York: Rinehart and Company, 1948.

155. Gerard Manley Hopkins, op. cit.

157. The Magic Barrel. New York: Farrar, Strauss, and Cudahy, 1950.

159. Poems: Bertolt Brecht (Later Svendborg Poems and Satire). John Willett and Ralph Manheim, eds. London: Methuen Publishing Company, 1976.

161. Fyodor Dostoevsky, op. cit.

163. New York: Holt, Rinehart and Winston, 1948.

165. Shakespeare, op. cit. (IV, i).

167. Henrik Ibsen, op. cit.

169. On the Gods and Other Essays. Buffalo: Prometheus Books, 1990.

171. The George Eliot Letters, Gordon Haight, ed. London: Yale University Press, 1978.

173. Poems by Emily Dickinson. Boston: Little, Brown and Company, 1957.

175. Source unknown.

177. The Wheel of Love and Other Stories. New York: Vanguard Press, 1965.

179. The Complete Poetical Works of Alexander Pope (Cambridge Edition). Boston: Houghton, Mifflin Company, 1903.

181. The Writings of John Burroughs, XIII. New York: Russell and Russell, 1968.

183. Flannery O'Connor, op. cit.

185. Star Points: Poems Selected by Mrs. Waldo Richards. Boston: Houghton Mifflin Company, 1921.

187. The World's Great Religious Poetry. Caroline Miles Hill, ed. New York: Macmillan Publishing Company, 1934.

189. J. Middleton Murry, ed. New York: Alfred A. Knopf, 1936.

191. Ivan Ilych and Hadji Muras and Other Stories, Louise and Aylmer Maude, eds. London: Oxford University Press, 1959.

193. By the Ionian Sea: Notes of a Ramble in Southern Italy (1901). London: Travellers Library, 1933.

195. The Collected Poetry of W. H. Auden. New York: Random House, 1945.

197. John Donne, op. cit.

Index

Invitation to Prayer 1
Rocking-Chair Thoughts 3
The Mother Love of Our Father 5
Being Part of the Body 7
Both…And 9
Bigger Spoons 11
A Hunger for Seriousness 13
My Green Trash Bag 15
The Two Options 17
Inescapable Associations 19
A World Grown Strange 21
The Widening Gyre 23
A Higher Perspective 25
The Creator Had a Plan 27
Weeding Out The Baobabs 29
Successful in Vain 31
It's Your Fault, God 33
The Kiss of Death 35
Seeing Our Real Faces 37
Tough Love 39
Too Dear a Price 41
The Beauty of Holiness 43
No Excuse at All 45
The Use of Our Lips 47
Scapegoat 49
The Unshared Experience 51
Tumbling Down Walls 53
Only More So 55
A Noble Earthquake! 57
God's Generosity 59
That Squalid Brood 61
When God Goes Hunting 63
Getting Bigger Inside 65
The Right Word 67
Proud Words 69
Cynic's Complaint 71
The Saintly Fool 73

A Good Name 75
Keeping the Faith 77
To Rise Again 79
When Death Shall Die 81
No Pat Answers 83
The Unavoidable Web 85
Real Freedom 87
Two of a Kind 89
"I Know of a Sleep" 91
The Place of Prayer 93
Dried Reeds and Cobwebs 95
Excuses, Excuses 97
Walking Openly 99
The Habit of Praise 101
Clean Spittoon 103
The Victory Achieved 105
How Short Our Life Is! 107
Plagued 109
Split Personality 111
The Setting Isn't Exclusive 113
Flirting with God 115
To Be Taken Seriously 117
The House of Prayer 119
More Money 121
Generations 123
The Blessing of Work 125
Strange Choices 127
All or Nothing 129
In Need of Praise 131
Big and Little Thieves 133
Walking on Water 135
That Which is Mine to Do 137
Keep Running 139
The Risk of Love 141
God's Wisdom or Ours? 143
Living Recklessly 145
Waters Rushing Back 147
Dilemma 149
A Reason for Discomfort 151
Monkey Ropes 153
In or Out of the Storm 155

Enamored of God? 157
Inescapable Consequences 159
His Example of Love 161
Mercy Too Late 163
The Quality of Mercy 165
Dispossessing Demons 167
Responsibility 169
In Deed and In Word 171
Sweet Singers 173
A Perpetual Court 175
A New Kind of Trap 177
The Danger of Familiarity 179
In the Stillness 181
The Greatest Message 183
Excelsior 185
A Treasured Gift 187
All in Order 189
The Mortal Exception 191
Patriotism or Chauvinism 193
After Christmas 195
Translation 197
List of Sources 199

To Order Copies

☎ **Telephone Orders:** Call 1-800-864-1648

✉ **Postal Orders:** LangMarc Publishing, PO Box 33817, San Antonio, Texas 78265-3817. USA.
Fax Orders: 210-822-5014

Echoings
soft cover $11.95

Quantity Discounts: 10% discount for 3-4 copies, 15% for 5-9 copies, 20% for 10 or more copies.

Shipping: UPS or Priority Mail: $3 for 1 or 2 books, 50¢ each additional book.

Book Rate: $1.50 for the first book and 50¢ each additional book. (Delivery two or three weeks)

Sales Tax: Texas residents only, add 7.25% (87¢ per book).

Send a Gift to a Friend: We will mail directly. Shipping cost to each address will be $3.00 UPS or $1.50 book rate.

Please send payment with order.

Books Cost: _____

Shipping: _____

Check Enclosed: _____

Name and Address for order delivery:

_____

_____

_____

_____